The Myth of German Engineering

Cars and Products that are Unsafe, Unreliable and Expensive to Maintain

By Joel D. Joseph

The Myth of German Engineering

Copyright © 2021 Joel D. Joseph. For rights and permissions write to Mr. Joseph at P.O. Box 12184, La Jolla, California 92039.

Dedication

This book is dedicated to my father, Harold Joseph, a lover of cars. He would never buy a German car because of the holocaust. Every time he saw the grill on a BMW it reminded him of Hitler's mustache.

Also by Joel D. Joseph

Legal Agreements in Plain English (1982)

How to Fight City Hall . . . The IRS, Banks, Corporations, Your Local Airport & Other Nuisances (1983)

Father/Son Book (1985)

The Glove Compartment Book (1985)

Employees Rights in Plain English (1985)

Black Mondays: Worst Decisions of the Supreme Court
(First Edition: 1987, Second Edition: 1989, Third Edition: 2008, Fourth Edition: 2014)
(Foreword by Justice Thurgood Marshall)

Made in the USA: The Complete Guide to America's Finest Products (1990-1996)

Fifty Ways to Create Jobs in the United States (2010)

All American Holiday Gift Guide (2011)

All American Back to School Guide (2011)

All American Office Products Guide (2012)

All American Wheels: Cars, Trucks and Motorcycles (2013)

Inequality in America: 10 Causes and 10 Cures (2014)

Table of Contents

1. Introduction 11
2. Dieselgate 29
3. Nickeled and Daimlered 38
4. Break My Wallet: The Ultimate Cash-Sucking Machine 56
5. Death by Porsche................................ 104
6. Audi 133
7. VW 150
8. Other German Products 160

About the Author 175

Chapter One

Introduction

German cars among worst for engine failures—

Auto Express (UK)

Many Americans tend to have a romantic attraction for German engineered cars. They flaunt them like the husband parades his trophy wife. They wax and polish them and want others to see them driving an expensive German luxury vehicle.

Vehicles such as BMW, Mercedes, Porsche and Audi carry a reputation for fine design and craftsmanship.

But when you look beyond the high price tag and the racy commercials, do these vehicles actually live up to their notoriety? In my humble opinion, they don't. In fact, many German automakers are living on the fumes of the past.

It has the heart of a BMW M5, the bones of an Audi RS 6 and the foul breath of a Seat Alhambra. No, this isn't one of Jeremy Clarkson's cheese-fuelled nightmares but a "Franken-car" assembled from the beastly parts of the world's most unreliable vehicles.

Warranty Direct, a third-party warranty provider, analyzed the data from 50,000 insurance policies to create its reliability index, which highlights the worst-performing cars in terms of mechanical reliability.

The Franken-car is a horrific amalgamation of unreliable components, including the engine of a BMW M5 made between 2004 and 2011, the axle and suspension from an Audi RS 6 (2002-11), the gearbox from a Jeep Grand Cherokee (2006-11) and the air-conditioning system from a Seat Alhambra (1996-2010).

According to Warranty Direct, its reliability index asses-ses the trustworthiness of vehicles by combining frequency of failure, average cost of repair, vehicle age and mileage. David Gerrans, the managing director, said: "This large variety of vehicles that goes into the concoction proves how typically reliable cars can be dragged down by one poorly performing part."

Audi, BMW and VW ranked in the bottom ten of a study into engine reliability. German-made cars are not as reliable as many believe, according to new research by Warranty Direct. Warranty Direct's claims data shows that Audi, BMW and Volkswagen all finished in the bottom 10 out of a total of 36 automakers. In fact, the only auto manufacturer whose cars had a worse engine failure rate than Audi was MG Rover. Mini wasn't much better, finishing third from bottom, while its parent company BMW came seventh from bottom. And, despite its reputation for rock-solid reliability, Volkswagen came ninth from last. Mercedes managed to outperform its fellow German brands with a respectable third-place finish.

Duncan McClure, Warranty Direct Managing Director, said that engine failures are the worst for motorists as they're the repairs that can lead to the highest costs because of the parts and hours of labor required to fix them: "The number of failures may be low compared to areas such as axle and suspension damage but engine repairs almost always result in costs reaching the thousands for motorists who aren't covered by a warranty."

Good Engineering Practices

There is no generally accepted definition of "Good Engineering Practices." It varies from industry to Industry. However, in general, good engineering includes the life cycle of the product (durability), safety and health ramifications and performance. The consensus of good engineering is:

1. Good performance;
2. Reliability;
3. Inexpensive maintenance; and
4. Safety.

Most German cars have good performance in terms of acceleration, handling and braking. The reliability of German vehicles has been on the decline, according to *Consumer Reports* and other testing organizations. Maintenance of German motor vehicles has always been expensive. *MyMechanic* found that BMW was the most expensive car to maintain by far, with Mercedes in second place.

The Porsche has been more reliable that most of the German vehicles. However, and this is a big however, Porsches are the most deadly cars on the road.

Overall, German cars are not reliable and are extremely expensive to maintain. Further, German cars are behind American and Japanese cars in electronics. Concerning electric vehicles, which will be the vehicles of the future, German auto companies are far behind American upstart Tesla.

Tesla in the Rear-View Mirror

"German automakers must invest more in electric vehicles and take on Elon Musk's Tesla Inc.," said Chancellor Angela Merkel's chief of staff Peter Altmaier. Altmeier has been Chief of Staff of the German Chancellery and as Federal Minister for Special Affairs since December 2013. Previously he was Federal Minister for the Environment, Nature Conservation and Nuclear Safety from May 2012 to December 2013. Altmaier is widely seen as one of Chancellor Angela Merkel's most trusted advisors

Peter Altmaier said he was thoroughly disappointed by German auto executives following the diesel-emissions scandal and that he was also thinking about the future of the 600,000 workers in the industry.

"When is our automobile industry, which is so good, actually going to be in a position to build a car that travels 50 kilometers further than a Tesla and costs 10,000 Euros less?" Altmaier said at a public forum in Berlin. "It must be possible to set this as a goal."

He referred to Tesla cars costing $100,000 with a range of 400 kilometers (250 miles). Tesla's German website shows a Model X Tesla with a range of as much as 417 kilometers selling for 91,250 Euros ($109,000). Tesla has added a more affordable vehicle, the Model 3 sedan, which starts at $35,000. The Model 3 is aimed squarely at the BMW 3, the Audi 4 and the Mercedes C class.

"If the [German] automobile industry doesn't grasp the fact that it has to invest more in electric vehicles, especially in cities, then it will be very hard to defend combustion engines -- gasoline and diesel -- over the long term," Altmaier said. "We must do all we can now, so that the best electric cars are built in Germany."

Der Spiegel reported, "The biggest cause for concern in the German auto industry is an American rival, Tesla.

Founded in 2003, it has achieved what the German manufacturers failed to do for years: build an electric car that many customers want." *Der Spiegel* is a German weekly news magazine, the equivalent of *Time* magazine in the United States. It is one of Europe's largest publications of its kind, with a weekly circulation of 840,000.

More than 450,000 consumers pre-ordered Tesla's new Model 3, and the company says that it is receiving another 1,800 orders a day. "Tesla now has a cult status that other brands can only dream of," says Karl-Thomas Neumann, a German auto expert and former head of Opel, GM's former German subsidiary. Tesla, as of 2019, was manufacturing 5,000 Model 3s per week, a rate of 250,000 per year.

Der Spiegel added, "The German carmakers' identity crisis comes at a convenient time for Tesla. While the U.S. company has been restrained in its public statements, Tesla managers speak off the record about 'illegal manipulations in the context of the diesel scandal.'"

Tesla smells an opportunity to gain a foothold in Germany, a country that has had relatively little affinity for U.S. cars in the past and is the home market of

Daimler, BMW and VW. The company has more than doubled its German sales in the first half of 2017, for a total of 2,000 vehicles. This is an impressive number for Germany, which lags behind other developed nations when it comes to electric cars.

In late 2016, Daimler, Ford, BMW and VW announced a joint initiative for rapid-charging stations. The project was scheduled to begin in 2017, with about 400 locations across Europe planned in the first phase. Nine months passed since the announcement and the number of charging stations is still zero. The first charging station is expected to open this year, allegedly with charging technology superior to Tesla's. By comparison, Tesla has already installed more than 6,300 of its so-called Superchargers worldwide. It aims increase that number to 10,000 by the end of the 2018.

Back to the 1960s

Back in the 1960s and 1970s, Germany built some great, reliable automobiles. In the good old days, *Consumer Reports* gushed about the reliability of Mercedes-Benz, BMW and Volkswagen vehicles. This helped to inflate German engineered cars to disproportionate levels. It's been that way ever since. Don't believe me? Take a look at these facts:

- **German cars lack innovation.** German automakers got fat and lazy living off of their nameplates. Meanwhile companies like Toyota have been pushing innovation through its hybrid technology and world-class safety features.

- **German cars aren't that reliable.** The whole point of having a car is to drive it. You can't do that when it's in the shop waiting on some expensive parts. When it comes to reliability, you can't go wrong with a Toyota or a Honda. Plus, Toyota and Honda OEM parts aren't as expensive as German auto parts.

- **There's a good chance your German engineered car wasn't even made in Germany.** Volkswagen manufactures some of its cars for the United States in Mexico. They're also building a plant for its Audi line of luxury cars in Mexico. Meanwhile, companies like Toyota and Honda are building manufacturing facilities in the USA.

These are just a few reasons we believe German engineered cars are overrated.

Autoguide.com reported:

> Likely you've heard the phrase "German engineering" more than a few times in your life and there's a popular misconception that it equals good reliability. German cars are well engineered, sometimes to be ama-zing performance machines and sometimes to be incredibly high-tech (and often both) but, Porsche aside, German cars don't have the best track record for reliability.

Part of the reason for the misconception about German engineering is that German automakers did, at one time, earn it. When *Consumer Reports* started its Long-Term Reliability Tests and Initial Quality Index tests way back in 1972, German brands like Volkswagen and Mercedes-Benz came out on top. The initial quality of even the lowly VW Beetle topped many domestic vehicles from Ford, Jeep, Pontiac and Mercury.

For a while afterwards, Mercedes and VW managed to stay near the top in reliability rankings. But their Japanese rivals weren't sitting idly-by. In the 1980s and 90s the most reliable models ended up coming from Honda, Toyota, Acura, Infiniti and Lexus.

"Back then, the cars like the Beetle were pretty simple. But then came stronger competition, the Japanese [automakers], especially Toyota and Honda got their problems per 100, down to a science," Said Gabriel Shenhar, an automotive engineer at *Consumer Reports*.

A Reputation Lost

Autoguide.com noted, "In the late '90s Mercedes had released the dismally unreliable M-Class SUV and the brand's initial quality scores have plummeted since. Other German brands had similar experiences. Even though they stayed at the forefront of new technology and engineering practices, their new gizmos were prone to failing."

"They're quick to adapt new technologies but rely on suppliers that supply these technologies and in a lot of cases what we see is problems with the electrical systems, the entertainment systems and other interface," said Shenhar of *Consumer Reports*.

According to *Consumer Reports*, Mercedes boosted its reliability a bit in 2011, but is still inconsistent. The same can be said for Mercedes' German competitors, Audi and BMW. In *Consumer Reports* last five annual reports, the last time these German brands have been above average in reliability was back in 2007. Since then, they've all slumped below the average in the industry.

Consumer Reports' Long-Term Reliability test documents a car's reliability over the course of three years, while the Initial Quality Index is based on consumer feedback from the first few months of a new cars ownership.

Consumer Reports also has a report card that ranks automakers based on their average car score, reliability score and the percentage of recommended vehicles. The average score for these carmaker report cards over the past five years (when they started the report cards) of the German brands doesn't crack 68/100, below the industry average and the competition from the top Japanese automakers.

These results are reflected in numbers released by J.D. Power & Associates as well. In both of the latest J.D. Power Surveys, the German brands can't match up to their luxury peers. In the most recent vehicle dependability survey, Mercedes-Benz only gets a four out of five, which is "Better than most" rating, while Audi and BMW get 3/5 or "About Average." Volkswagen falls below average with 2/5, what J.D. Power describes as "The Rest." Porsche is also ranked "Better than most" in J.D. Power's dependability survey, which give Mercedes-Benz some nice company. It's important to note that only one carmaker had a score of 5/5, and that's Lexus.

Nothing changes in J.D. Power's Initial Quality rankings. Mercedes and Porsche have 4/5 ratings, BMW and Audi get just 3/5 and VW only achieves 2/5. Lexus tops that ranking as well with a 5/5. The J.D. Power ratings are based on consumer surveys. Initial Quality is measured after 90 days of a new car's purchase. Vehicle Dependability Ratings are surveys based on the past 12 months of original owners of three-year old cars.

Poor Rankings Are About More than Quality

Some of the reasons why German cars struggle in J.D. Power's rankings in the past are entirely trivial and are not related to actual vehicle quality at all says Karl Brauer from *Total Car Score*. "German cars didn't offer cup holders for years, and while this isn't a mechanical failure it was often noted as a dissatisfaction point for buyers on J.D. Power and *Consumer Reports* surveys, and this drove down their scores" said Brauer. "Most German cars (even Porsches) now have cup-holders because the manufacturers realized they were suffering in terms of owner satisfaction scores by not having them," he added. The same thing could be said about some of the complicated technologies and infotainment systems like BMW's first generation iDrive system.

Good Performance, Poor Reliability

Along with these more trivial complaints, like a lack of drink holders, and technology issues, Shenhar of *Consumer Reports,* tells us that German automakers, by their own admission, sometimes come up short because of their singular focus on performance. When and if they cut costs, the likely areas that will get cheaper quality parts will be with some of the stuff the customer might not notice. "They are susceptible to cost-cutting and anywhere they can, in the hopes that the customer won't know, they use suppliers that will deliver and sometimes won't," says Shenhar.

While the phrase "German Engineering" has become synonymous with reliability, Shenhar suggests it should more accurately be a reference to performance. And in regards to performance, there's little doubt they have some high standards. In fact, looking away from initial quality and reliability, German vehicles rank quite well.

Dangerous Cars

More threatening than a poor repair record is a car that is downright dangerous to drive. The chapter on Porsche finds that it is the most dangerous car in the world. The design of the Porsche is much like that of the Chevrolet Corvair that was skewered in Ralph Nader's *Unsafe at Any Speed*. Both of these death traps place the engine behind the rear wheels making the car exceptionally difficult to maneuver.

The chapter on BMW demonstrates that Bimmers are prone to catch on fire more than other cars. Many BMWs have self-ignited when parked on the street or in a garage. Safety recalls are also exceptionally common for most German cars. The author reviewed hundreds of U.S. National Highway Traffic Safety recalls as well as scores of class action lawsuits against German automakers.

Antitrust Violations

German car manufacturing giants Volkswagen, Daimler and BMW illegally colluded to hinder competition on emission cleaning technology, the European Commission ruled on April 5, 2019. The initial findings from an investigation by the EU's antitrust regulators came nearly two years after authorities carried out raids on their headquarters.

What the European Commission Found

The European Antitrust Commission Found:

- From 2006 to 2014, the three German automakers conspired to limit the development and roll-out of emission cleaning technology for passenger cars sold in Europe.

- The talks were aimed at restricting competition and "breached EU antitrust rules."

- Two types of technology specifically were restricted: one to reduce nitrogen oxide emissions from diesel cars, and another to reduce harmful particulate matter from petrol engine cars.

- The companies "denied consumers the opportunity to buy less polluting cars" despite the technology being available.

Colluding "not to improve their products"

EU Commissioner Margrethe Vestager, who is in charge of competition policy, said EU antitrust authorities were concerned that VW, BMW and Daimler Benz purposefully restricted their customer's access to the best technology.

"Companies can cooperate in many ways to improve the quality of their products. However, EU competition rules do not allow them to collude on exactly the opposite: not to improve their products, not to compete on quality," Vestager said. A Daimler spokesperson said that it was cooperating with investigators, but that the company does not expect to be fined as a result of the probe.

These preliminary findings were the latest emissions scandal to hit the German auto industry. VW, in particular, has been hit hard by the 2015 "Dieselgate" emissions cheating scandal, where the company admitted to installing a device to cheat air pollution tests in 11 million vehicles around the world. BMW,

Daimler and VW were also heavily criticized in 2018 for paying for animal tests that exposed monkeys to toxic diesel fumes.

The European Commission said it has notified the companies of its initial findings. The German automakers will have a chance to respond. Antitrust regulators emphasized that the investigation is not yet over. Should VW, BMW and Daimler be found guilty of violating antitrust rules, however, the Commission can impose a fine of up to 10% of each company's annual worldwide sales.

Chapter Two

Dieselgate:

Volkswagen, Porsche, Mercedes and Audi Cheated on Emissions

"As a part of Volkswagen Group, Audi played a central role in developing and installing illegal software in 11 million diesel cars in order to trick emissions tests."

--Wolfgang Kerler,
noted German automotive expert.

In 1968 Volkswagen introduced the first on-board computer system in the world with scanning capability, in their fuel-injected Type 3 models. That was fifty years ago. For the first years of the on-board computer

Volkswagen led the automotive world in computer technology. It did not take long for Volkswagen to use this technology for evil purposes.

In 1974 Volkswagen paid a $120,000 fine to settle a complaint filed by the Environmental Protection Agency over the use of so-called defeat devices that disabled certain pollution-control systems. The complaint said the use of the devices violated the U.S. Clean Air Act.

In 2011, Greenpeace began criticizing Volkswagen's opposition to legislation requiring tighter controls on CO_2 emissions and energy efficiency, and launched an adver-tising campaign parodying VW's series of *Star Wars*-based commercials.

In 1991, the California Air Resources Board (CARB) requires that all new vehicles sold in California in 1991 and newer vehicles have some basic OBD capability. These requirements are generally referred to as "OBD-I," though this name is not applied until the introduction of OBD-II. The data link connector and its position are not standardized, nor is the data protocol.

In 1996, the OBD-II specification is made mandatory for all cars manufactured in the United States to be sold in the United States. In 2001, The European Union made EOBD mandatory for all gasoline (petrol) vehicles sold in the European Union. Effective in 2003, the European Union made EOBD mandatory for all diesel cars sold in the European Union

The Volkswagen emissions scandal began in September 2015, when the United States Environmental Protection Agency (EPA) issued a notice of violation of the Clean Air Act to German automaker Volkswagen Group. The agency had found that Volkswagen had intentionally programmed turbocharged direct injection (TDI) diesel engines to activate their emissions controls only during laboratory emissions testing which caused the vehicles' NOx output to meet U.S. standards during regulatory testing, but emit up to 40 times more NOx in real-world driving. Volkswagen deployed this programming software in about eleven million cars worldwide, including 500,000 in the United States, in model years 2009 through 2015.

As a part of Volkswagen Group, Audi played a central role in developing and installing illegal software in 11 million diesel cars in order to trick emissions tests. On September 18, 2015, the US Environmental Protection Agency informed the public about VW's and Audi's violation of the Clean Air Act, causing government agencies around the world to launch investigations.

Dieselgate became the biggest scandal to rock the car industry in decades, and within three years, Volkswagen Group was forced to pay $30 billion to settle the case. The sum is likely to rise by several billion dollars.

While they are busy emphasizing their commitment to electric vehicles, German carmakers are still scrambling to contain the fallout of Dieselgate: executives are held in prison; investors are suing for billions; the EU Commission is investigating VW, Daimler, and BMW for collusion; and the once cozy relationship with Angela Merkel's government has cracked severely.

Rupert Stadler, the CEO of Audi was held in custody in a Bavarian prison for three months for his role in Diesel-gate. Not only is he suspected of having made false statements to authorities, prosecutors think that he also tried to manipulate important witnesses.

Stadler was the sixth Volkswagen Group executive to be imprisoned or Dieselgate-related alleged crimes. The list of suspects from VW, Audi, and Porsche has grown to as many as 70 names, which translates into a lot of work for Volkswagen's lawyers.

But Volkswagen is facing another problem. In September, 2019, investors filed a $10 billion lawsuit in Braunschweig, Germany against the company, seeking compensation for the up to 37 percent hit to Volkswagen's share price following the revelations by the EPA. They argue that VW failed to meet its duty to warn shareholders about the scandal's financial impact. "I expect the lawsuit to be successful," Ferdinand Dudenhöffer, professor of Automotive Economics at the University of Duisburg-Essen, said. "Including this case and all other pending lawsuits, I assume that Volkswagen will have to pay another $15 billion in fines."

Volkswagen isn't the only automaker in chaos. Daimler is having some serious diesel-related trouble, too. In Europe, the company recently had to recall 700,000 Mercedes-Benz diesel cars over irregularities with their emissions control software. While the German government threatened the company with a $4 billion fine, it is still unclear if Daimler will actually have to pay. By comparison, BMW has little to worry about. Although dozens of prosecutors and police officers raided the company's headquarters in Munich this spring (some-thing that happened to Daimler and VW much earlier), they didn't find evidence of any major crimes. According to a recent report by daily Süddeutsche Zeitung that cited numbers of Germany's Ministry of Transport, about 8,000 BMW diesel cars were equipped with inadmissible systems to shut down emission controls. The company says this was caused by "human error." In the end, BMW might only have to pay a $12 million fine.

The European Commission is Intensifying its Investigation

In addition to these individual cases, there is a broader set of problems that encompasses the entire German auto industry. Just in time for Dieselgate's third anniversary, the European Commission announced that it is intensifying its investigation into whether VW, Audi, Daimler, BMW, and Porsche colluded on diesel emissions starting as far back as in the early 1990s. They are accused of having formed an illegal "cartel" which laid the foundation for Dieselgate. The Commission carried out inspections at the premises of BMW, Daimler, VW, and Audi in October 2017. "If proven, this collusion may have denied consumers the opportunity to buy less polluting cars, despite the technology being available to the manufacturers," said

Margrethe Vestager, the European Commissioner for Competition.

Dieselgate has led to an upheaval in Germany's politics as well. For decades, car executives cultivated friendly rela-tionships with German lawmakers. Things were down-right cozy. Before Dieselgate, Germany's most powerful car lobbyist started his letters to the chancellor with "Dear Angela." If other EU member states, the EU Commission, or the European Parli-ament were pushing for stricter regulations, car manufacturers could always rely on German officials to water down new European rules. Experts conclude that politicians are partly to blame for Dieselgate. "German politicians always thought they were helping the car industry by being soft on regulations and keeping their eyes shut," Dudenhöffer said.

Now, politicians and manufacturers will pay the price for their close relationship. Most German voters now think the government was too lenient on Volkswagen, Daimler, and BMW. Thanks to industry lobbying and German interventions, European rules for the emission of nitrogen oxides (NOx) are full of so many loopholes that virtually all diesel cars emit more pollutants into the environment while on the street than they do at testing facilities. While not illegal, these super-polluting vehicles have made the air in many German cities much dirtier than allowed under EU standards.

"For years, the German government has been reprimanded by the EU Commission," Dudenhöffer said, "but it has never done anything about it." To improve air quality, courts have banned older diesel cars from several German cities or parts of them. Hamburg, Frankfurt, and Stuttgart were the first to announce these restrictions. "In the end, we will probably get diesel bans in 20 German cities," Dudenhöffer said.

Needless to say that this won't go down well with many German voters as millions of them own diesel cars. To prevent driving bans, the government is finally thinking about obligatory hardware updates at the manufacturers' expense to reduce NOx emissions in older diesel cars. Environmentalists have been calling for this for months, but the government didn't want to impose it on the car industry. It only demanded software updates that are less effective, but much cheaper.

The threat of driving bans is already causing the market share of diesel vehicles to collapse. In the first half of 2017, over 41 percent of new cars in Germany were diesel. In 2018 the number went down to 32 percent, according to new research by the University of Duisburg-Essen.

The era of diesel cars, which are particularly important for German manufacturers, is coming to an end much faster than Volkswagen, Daimler, and BMW probably planned. However, as consumers in China and the United States have quickly forgotten the affair, German automakers are still making more money than ever. The move into electric vehicles, then, is both image rehab and financial necessity — because it turns out Germans have fallen out of love with diesel cars.

Chapter Three
Nickeled and Daimlered

"The Mercedes is a rear-wheel-drive car and is one the lousiest snow cars known to man. Surpassed in lack of snow ability only by your average BMW."

--Click & Clack, syndicated auto column

Volkswagen isn't the only automaker in chaos. Daimler is having some serious diesel-related trouble, too. In Europe, the company recently had to recall 700,000 Mercedes-Benz diesel cars over irregularities with their emissions control software. While the German government threatened the company with a $4 billion fine, it is still unclear if Daimler will actually have to pay.

The good news is that the Mercedes is not the most expensive car to maintain. That dubious honor belongs to BMW. According to *YourMechanic,* BMW is the most expensive car to maintain, costing nearly twice as much as the Mercedes. *Your Mechanic* has a large database of maintenance on cars. According to *Your Mechanic,* the average cost to maintain a BMW for ten years is $17,800. Mercedes' cost for the same period is $12,900.

Safety First

I always thought of the Mercedes as a safe car. But this is no longer the case. The U.S. Insurance Institute for High-way Safety gave the Mercedes C-Class a score of "poor" in its small overlap frontal crash test, despite receiving good marks on the other IIHS tests. Neither the side curtain nor side torso airbags deployed in the test, and the dummy's foot was stuck beneath the brake pedal. The pedal had to be cut off to free the foot. IIHS also noted the seat belt allowed for too much forward movement, with the head at risk of hitting the A-pillar, which is the vertical support near the driver's seat.

Consumer Reports presented 10 cars that earned their lowest Overall Score in each vehicle class, basing their ratings on road-test score, reliability, owner satisfaction, and safety, including government and insurance industry crash-test results. One Mercedes made the list of the ten most dangerous cars of 2016.

All of the vehicles below earned low safety scores from *Consumer Reports* which means they performed poorly on crash tests by the National Highway Traffic Safety Administration and the Insurance Institute for Highway Safety. Additionally, *Consumer Reports* considers the presence of standard advanced safety technology in each vehicle they rate, and those without adequate safety features earn lower scores.

Mercedes-Benz CLA 250

Why it's unsafe:

- IIHS: the vehicle's headlights earned a "poor" rating
- Consumer Reports Road-Test score: 64

Reliability and owner satisfaction are well below average, says *Consumer Reports*.

Mercedes-Benz Recalls
Takata Airbag Recall Lawsuit

As of 2017, the National Highway Traffic Safety Administration (NHTSA) reported that about one million Mercedes-Benz vehicles are subject to recall due to defective and potentially deadly airbags manufactured by the Takata Corporation, which have already claimed several lives and resulted in hundreds of serious injuries. This is a direct consequence of the U.S. nationwide Mercedes-Benz Takata Airbag Recall, which so far, along with the recalls of several other auto manufacturers, affects approximately 42-million vehicles, making it the largest recall in U.S history.

The Mercedes' airbags that are being recalled are due to Takata's unsafe use of ammonium nitrate, a chemical compound commonly used in explosive devices which, after exposure to moisture in areas with high heat, can destabilize over time and explode, sending metal shrapnel into the vehicle (even in minor accidents). Coupled with a defective design in the metal housing chamber, this creates a very serious safety issue that can result in blindness, wounds, lacerations, disfigurement, and even death.

Although the airbags are dangerous, replacing the *Takata airbags in Mercedes Benz* vehicles will be difficult to accomplish in a timely manner due to the millions of other vehicles also subject to the Takata airbag recall. Even worse, some Mercedes-Benz vehicles will only receive an "interim remedy," in which the recalled airbag device be replaced with the exact same defective com-ponents, the only difference being a "fresher" ammonium nitrate. Although this does "temporarily" decrease the likelihood of a deadly explosion, Mercedes-Benz will again need to recall these airbags as they will ultimately be just as dangerous as the ones they replaced.

The NHTSA has already ordered that Takata phase out the use of their defective airbags by 2020, and has announced that Mercedes and any other manufacturers performing an interim remedy, will need to replace these temporary fixes before their vehicles are actually safe to drive.

The following is a list of Mercedes-Benz vehicles that are likely to have a Takata airbag installed:

- 2009-2010 **ML-Class**

- 2009-2012 **GL-Class**
- 2009-2012 **R-Class**
- 2007-2008 **SLK-Class**
- 2010-2015 **GLK-Class**
- 2011-2015 **SLS-Class**
- 2010-2011 **E-Class**
- 2011-2017 **E-Class Cabriolet**
- 2010-2017 **E-Class Coupe**
- 2005-2014 **C-Class**
- 2010-2017 **Sprinter**

Takata may not be the only company liable for installing the defective and deadly airbags. In fact, Mercedes-Benz installed Takata's airbags in their 2016 and 2017 Mercedes Benz E-Class vehicles, even after the deadly effects were discovered in 2015. Instead of investing to redesign their airbag module, Mercedes Benz decided to continue using ammonium nitrate airbags in these vehicles until they are forced to recall them again in the future.

Tail Lights

Mercedes-Benz USA, LLC (Mercedes) is recalling certain model year 2008-2011 C300, C300 4Matic, C350, and C63 AMG vehicles manufactured January 26, 2007, through July 13, 2011. In the affected vehicles, a poor electrical ground connection may result in the dimming or failure of the tail lights.

Dimming or failure of the tail lights reduces the ability to warn other motorists of the driver's intentions of stop-ping or turning, increasing the risk of a crash.

Electrical System Software

Mercedes-Benz USA, LLC (MBUSA) recalled certain 2016 AMG GT-S, GLC300, CLA250 and GLE300d 4Matic vehicles, 2013 C250, E350 BlueTec and G63 AMG vehicles, 2008-2014 C300 vehicles, 2013-2014 C300 4Matic and ML350 4Matic vehicles, 2009 C350 vehicles, 2014 CLS550, E350 4Matic, E350 Coupe 4Matic, E350 Wagon 4Matic, GLK350 and SL550 vehicles, 2012 CLS550 4Matic vehicles, 2012-2016 E350 vehicles, 2016-2017 GL450 4Matic vehicles, 2012-2014 ML350 4Matic BlueTec vehicles, 2015 S550, S550 4Matic and C300 4Matic Sedan vehicles,

2015-2016 C300 Sedan vehicles, and 2017 SL63 AMG vehicles. Various control units on these vehicles may have been updated with incorrect software, potentially affecting the correct deployment of the air bags in the event of a crash.

If the air bags do not deploy as intended in the event of a crash, there would be an increased risk of injury in the event of a crash.

Recall for Fire Hazard

About 308,000 Mercedes-Benz vehicles across the United States were recalled because of a potential fire hazard. The problem has been linked to 35 car fires in the country. Mercedes determined that there's an issue with an engine part that can cause an electrical fire.

The recall will include certain C and E-Class vehicles, as well as CLA, GLA and GLC vehicles. "This situation typically occurs in the rare situation where a vehicle is stranded in a significant amount of standing water and the engine stalls and cannot be restarted on the first try," a Mercedes spokesperson said. The recall is voluntary, and Mercedes said the National Highway Traffic Safety Administration -- which helps companies carry out recalls -- has been notified.

Firefighters dousing a two-week old S-Class luxury sedan, which caught fire in Rottach-Egern, south of Munich.

Sunroof Problems

Mercedes-Benz is recalling 744,852 vehicles in the United States because of faulty sunroofs. The recall was triggered because the glass panel could detach from the vehicle. A decade of Mercedes are affected by this recall, spanning from model years 2001 to 2011.

Is Mercedes a Reliable Car?

Consumer Reports is a good place to start when looking at how reliable a product is, and a car is no different. *Consumer Reports* has been carrying out long-term reliability tests since 1972 and once placed Mercedes as number one for reliability. However, their assessment has become a little more *scathing* since 1999, when Mer-cedes launched their first ever SUV. Since then, the brand has fared near average on their reliability charts.

In fact, ever since 2007, Mercedes have not scored above average by *Consumer Reports* in regards to reliability. In 2014, *Consumer Reports* reported that the Mercedes CLA was not only the most unreliable Mercedes in the Auto Reliability Survey, but 140% worse than the average car on the road. Has much changed for 2019?

Consumer Reports ran their annual Car Brands Reliability survey for 2018, and Mercedes came in 14th place. According to the survey, Mercedes cars are currently more unreliable than the likes of Volkswagen and Tesla, but more reliable than Porsche, Infiniti and their closest rivals BMW and Audi.

According to the same survey, the GL3 model is the least reliable model Mercedes, while the E-Class model is the most reliable. Overall, Mercedes was given an average reliability score of 47, which ranks as fairly reliable.

J.D Power's dependability study tells a similar story, with Mercedes sitting mid-table in their 2018 league table. Lexus sits at the top with 99 problems per 100 vehicles, while Mercedes has 147 problems per 100 vehicles.

Warranty Directs findings are a bit more negative. According to its research in 2017, Mercedes are the fifth likeliest car to break down. They have a 25% breakdown rate, as well as a $750 (£560) average payout claim – which is quite high.

German cars are "the world's worst lemons," reports the car review website dogandlemon.com. Its Editor, Clive Matthew-Wilson, says: "New Zealand motorists often think they are getting an upmarket vehicle when they buy a European brand. However, the opposite is true: European vehicles are generally poorly built, unreliable and expensive to fix."

Matthew-Wilson quoted a recent car reliability survey by the giant English consumer organization Which? Of the 34 makes surveyed, Volkswagen was 15th, BMW was 18th, Audi was 20th, Mercedes was tenth.

Matthew-Wilson adds:

> Because many small European models are available with super-efficient engines, customers are buying these cars believing that they'll save money. In fact the opposite is likely to be true: the money these customers save on fuel is

likely to be a drop in the ocean compared to the high cost of ser-vicing and repairs, coupled with a shocking depreciation.

Virtually all reliability surveys say the same thing: European brands may look cool, but they're the pits to own.

Next to their house, a car is most people's most expensive purchase, yet the majority of car buyers purchase their vehicles with-out the faintest idea of what they are getting themselves into. If the New Zealanders who buy European cars knew the track record of these so-called prestige brands, they'd prob-ably never buy them.

Why are Mercedes Unreliable?

Consumer Reports, J.D. Power and Warranty Direct establish that Mercedes aren't very reliable. Why is this the case?

The reason why Mercedes and many other premium brands have such a poor reliability record? It usually comes down to the fact that they use so much new technology.

Mercedes cars come *packed* with new technology, and it's often the technology lets them down. Mercedes are clearly luxury vehicles, but their "high-tech," like the "complex infotainment system," is its achilles heel.

Consumer Reports has consistently scored Mercedes highly on its implementation of new technology. But it relies on suppliers to implement this technology and sometimes that comes with faults.

An automotive engineer at *Consumer Reports*, Gabriel Shenhar, said, "Mercedes is quick to adapt new technologies but rely on supplies that supply those technologies, and in a lot of cases what we see is problems with the electrical system, the entertainment system and the other interface."

Mercedes actually produce fantastic engines. As long as you maintain your Mercedes and get its oil changed exactly when you should, your car should hold up – in theory. The problem is that its overuse of technology decreases reliability.

All German premium brands are dogged by reliability issues. But which one is the most unreliable? It's a bit of a redundant question. J.D Power puts Mercedes and Audi higher than BMW in terms of overall dependability – but *Which?* ranks BMW and Audi higher than Mercedes.

Consumer Reports ranks BMW higher in its reliability table, at 5th place, in 2016 – but in 2018, Mercedes is ranked higher. The truth is, all three brands are as reliable – or as unreliable as each other, and their positions in the tables change each year.

Which Mercedes are the Most Reliable?

As with any brand, some Mercedes models are more dependable than others.

The following are based on the J.D Power predicted dependability score and achieve a ranking of above average or higher:

- 2015 GLK-Class
- 2009 SLK-Class
- 2010 C-Class

So, a mixture of classes and years, but it's good to know if you're looking at a secondhand Mercedes. Also, this will give you an idea of how reliable the newer versions of these cars are.

Which Mercedes are the Least Reliable?

So, what about the least reliable models? The following have a predicted reliability score of below average:

- 2009 S-Class
- 2015 GL-Class
- 2009 E-Class

Considering all of the reviews, is the Mercedes-Benz reliable? Their engine reliability is one of the highest in the market, but it is let down by their use of such new and advanced technology.

Diesels

Every Mercedes-Benz car sold in Britain from 2011-2017 was recalled by the German vehicle giant Daimler amid a scandal over "faked" emission results. Owners of nearly every model made by the firm will be asked to return their cars so the engines can be adjusted to reduce the amount of pollutants they emit.

It follows the launch of an investigation by the German authorities in 2017 into allegations of fraud and criminal advertising by employees of the firm relating to the possible manipulation of exhaust controls in cars with diesel engines.

As part of the investigation hundreds of police officers and prosecutors searched Daimler sites across Germany. The company has said it is cooperating with the investigation.

It comes amid continued scrutiny of the company's emissions systems by the German government and calls for bans on diesel engines in the country's cities. There have been calls for a ban on diesel cars in some German cities because of concerns about levels of nitrogen oxide they emit.

Daimler's announcement came just hours after the regional government in the company's home region of Baden-Wuerttemburg agreed to abandon proposals to restrict diesels if older diesels could be mechanically fixed to pollute less. The recall will have an impact on hundreds of thousands of Daimler vehicles, including the popular C-class and E-class Mercedes-Benz, sold in Britain.

In 2015 alone 145,254 Mercedes-Benz cars were sold in the UK, up from 124,419 the previous year - the vast majority of them diesel engines.

Dieter Zetsche, Daimler's chief executive officer, said on Tuesday: "The public debate about diesel engines is creating uncertainty. We have therefore decided on additional measures to reassure drivers of diesel cars and to strengthen confidence in diesel technology."

But the company says this does not spell the end of its production of diesel engine cars and vans. Mr. Zetsche added: "We are convinced that diesel engines will continue to be a fixed element of the drive-system mix, not least due to their low CO_2 emissions."

Daimler customers in the UK - along those in Europe - will shortly begin receiving letters from the firm inviting them to book their vehicles into an approved dealership in order for the work to be carried out. It will take around an hour and will be free of charge.

Daimler has been offering a similar voluntary recall on compact diesel cars and V-Class vans since March.

It will now cover nearly all vehicles made under the EU5 emissions standards - introduced in 2011 - and the more recent EU6 emissions standards and begin in the next few weeks. The required adjustment to the operation of the engine is estimated to take around an hour.

The reputation of diesel cars was hit by the admission by Daimler's competitor Volkswagen in 2015 that it had equipped vehicles with illegal software that meant they passed emissions tests, only to exceed limits in everyday driving.

The latest recall follows its decision in March to recall about 75,000 Mercedes-Benz cars in the UK in March because of the risk of fire.

Daimler recalled one million cars worldwide after 51 fires were reported in vehicles It said the fault affects the fuse in some of its A, B, C, and E-class cars as well as its CLA, GLA and GLC vehicles and could cause them to overheat in "unique conditions." The German company said these conditions would occur during the starting of the car.

Chapter Four

Break My Wallet: The Ultimate Unreliable Driving Machine

"So my question today is: what the hell happened? Where did BMW go wrong? When did the once almighty BMW, the ambassador of cool, the diplomat of debonair finally go off into the deep end and lose the plot?"

--Doug DeMuro, Auto expert

They're nicknamed, **Break My Wallet** for a reason. According to *YourMechanic,* BMW is the most expensive car to maintain, costing fifty percent more than the second-place Mercedes. *Your Mechanic* has a large database of maintenance on cars. According to *Your Mechanic,* the cost to maintain a Bimmer for ten years is $17,800. Mercedes' cost for the same period is $12,900.

I spoke with a homeless man in La Jolla, California recently. He mentioned that he used to own a BMW. Maybe the cost of owning a BMW put him out on the street. Many people buy them for the "prestige" and wind up paying a large price to keep them running.

According to *YourMechanic,* BMWs have a propensity not to start. BMW they found have four times the problem with not starting as the average car. No matter how well a car performs when it is running, not starting is surely a performance and safety issue.

The Decline of the BMW

Consumer Reports has said that BMW, as well as their fellow German brands, put most of their focus on performance. This can come at a cost to reliability. Gabriel Shenhar, senior automotive engineer at *Con-*

sumer *Reports*, said that "They are susceptible to cost-cutting anywhere they can in the hope that the customer won't know, they use suppliers that will deliver and sometimes they won't."

Shenhar points out that a common gripe people have with BMW is that they are sometimes guilty of using plastics instead of more durable materials. Another com-mon complaint is that the complex electronics BMW implement in their models are prone to breaking down.

While the phrase "German Engineering" has become synonymous with reliability, Shenhar suggests it should more accurately be a reference to performance. When *Consumer Reports* started its Long-Term Reliability Tests and Initial Quality Index tests way back in 1972, German brands came out on top. In *Consumer Reports* last five annual reports, the last time these German brands have been above average in reliability was way back in 2007. Since then, they've all slumped below the average in the industry.

JD Power conducts annual reliability surveys. BMW rates three out of five, which is about average.

Doug DeMuro started his career in the auto industry at Porsche. After he graduated from Emory University he put his Economics degree to good use at Porsche's North American corporate headquarters, where he quickly rose to become the youngest manager in the company's history. DeMuro's work has been featured in a multitude of magazine publications and websites, including *AutoTrader.com, Jalopnik,* and *The Week.*

DeMuro wrote:

> Twenty years ago, BMW was the coolest automaker in the world. I know this because I – as a young lad of less than ten, growing up in the 1990s – desperately wanted my father to purchase a BMW. And he – as a rational, middle-aged man in his 40s – ended up in a Camry with cloth seats and a tape player. He wasn't the BMW type. He wasn't cool enough. Back then, few were.
>
> Twenty years later, here we are: the BMW of now. Gran Coupes. Gran Turismos. xDrive35i. Sports activity vehicles. iDrive. And a front-wheel drive electric car with a trim level called Giga

World. I swear that if a meeting ever took place between the two BMW eras, 1990s BMW would punch 2010s BMW in the face and give it a wedgie while it was lying on the ground.

Things have gotten so bad that there's kind of a running understanding among modern car enthusiasts that BMW has turned to crap. It's like when you're on a boat, and you're rapidly taking on water. Nobody says you're taking on water, but it's plain to see: there you are, in the middle of the ocean, with minnows swimming around your ankles.

Essentially, the problems are as follows: the cars are bloated. The segments make no sense. The names are bizarre. And what the hell is the 2 Series Active Sports Tourer? Is that a joke? Are we supposed to pretend that thing simply doesn't exist?

So my question today is: what the hell happened? Where did BMW go wrong? When did the once almighty BMW, the ambassador of cool, the diplomat of debonair (eh? EH?!), finally go off into the deep end and lose the plot? I'll give you my theory – and below, you can submit yours.

My theory: it wasn't a car that caused BMW to lose it. It was an all-out, no-holds-barred sales-chasing mentality; the kind of mentality Chrysler has with the rental fleets. I think it was this strategy – and not the vehicles themselves – that led to the decline of BMW. Essentially, it was the moment the automaker went from "How can we make this car cooler?" to "Why don't we have a vehicle in the all-wheel drive rhombus segment?"

Of course, the "sell everything" mentality dramatically affected the products. Out went the careful styling decisions and the restrained lineup; in came segment-busting products and low-payment lease deals. The 3 Series grew huge. The X1 came into existence. And the 5 Series went from "desirable and stealthy" to "enormous and anonymous."

But in my opinion, none of that would've happened if BMW had remained happy with the status quo: build cool cars, and sell a lot of them. Not tons of them, mind you. Not zillions. Not eleven crossovers and twelve variants of the 3 Series. But enough cars to generate a big profit while retaining the "cool guy" image.

BMW has also had problems with electrical and electronic issues. Some of the electrical defects have caused a rash of car fires. The electronic issues include faulty navigation systems and cell-phone links. BMW has just not kept up with state-of-the-art electronics.

Freddy "Tavarish" Hernandez is a contributing writer for the motoring blog *Jalopnik*. He also runs the website APiDA Online where he writes articles and guides about cars. Hernandez also repairs cars, especially BMWs. Mr. Hernandez wrote:

> Few marques command as much respect from people who crave performance as BMW, and the M line of cars in par-

ticular are some of the most desirable and most powerful vehicles around. However, there's a closely guarded secret that no respected publication would ever broach, and it's that all BMW engines are monumental piles of unreliable garbage.

It's no secret that German reliability is a myth. The likelihood of an average German car making it 10 years without several un-planned roadside mishaps approaches the same probability of you waking up tomorrow as Katy Perry.

Hernandez said that over the last few years, he bought and sold some of BMW's most desirable consumer cars. He has owned them, driven them, and most importantly, worked on them - five in total, ranging from the M3 to the M5, the high performance BMW models.

He said that, "I can tell you that every single time I started any engine with a BMW badge on it, there was the same sense of concerned dread that the stereotypical bomb squad guys got in '80s action flicks. . . . . It's a literal time bomb."

Hernandez pointed out an unique problem in the M3 in which the nut that held the sprocket driving the oil pump would *fall off*. "Yes, the one thing that made sure your engine was oiled properly would simply fall apart, because it wasn't torqued down properly from the factory." He added, "and that's the *reliable* one. If you move to more late model stuff, the situation gets a bit more dire."

He pointed out that the E46 M3, for example featured a 333-horsepower naturally aspirated inline six-cylinder engine. "That was more unreliable than an AA meeting sponsored by Miller Lite. These engines were plagued with connecting rod bearing failures, issues with the variable cam timing (VANOS), crankcase ventilation failures, hard starting, and their cooling systems were made of plastic and sealed, ensuring catastrophic failure where scalding hot coolant would shoot out of your engine bay, overheating your engine, at which point your head gasket would blow."

He noted that the same goes for every M-branded car that BMW has made in the last decade, and these problems are well-documented. He said, "The E60 M5's V10 will chew through its rod bearings in less than 60,000 miles and has rampant and costly SMG pump failures.

The E92 M3 will also devour its rod bearings in short order."

BMW Flambé

ABC News reported that BMWs were catching on fire all over the country. This led to a class action lawsuit and a massive recall.

Scores of parked BMWs have burst into flames. Vehicle owners and fire departments across the country asked BMW to explain how some parked cars could suddenly burst into flames. An *ABC News* investigation airing on Good Morning America, *World News Tonight with* David Muir and *Nightline* reported dozens of incidents in which the luxury cars caught fire even though owners reported they had parked their cars and turned them off.

After initially saying they were unaware of any such incidents, a BMW spokesman said the company had investigated the fires brought to its attention by *ABC News* and has "not seen any pattern" related to a "product defect."

For one owner, Bill Macko, BMW wasn't just a car, it was an identity. The 55-year-old small business owner says he had bought seven luxury vehicles from the German automaker since 2000. He was a dues-paying member of the BMW Car Club of America, so he read BMW mag-azines, carried BMW luggage and wore BMW clothes. He was such a BMW enthusiast that he became, he says, a kind of unofficial brand ambassador, introducing so many new customers to the local BMW dealership that the salesmen occasionally cut him a check for his services.

"I was an aficionado," Macko said. "I had brought so many people on board to BMWs, it was crazy. Everybody knew that I loved them so much ... I mean, I lived the product, you know?"

On the night of Dec. 1, 2015, however, Macko says his 2008 BMW X5 suddenly and inexplicably caught-fire as it sat parked in his garage in Olney, Maryland. Macko's wife had just returned from a short drive, parked the car and turned it off. She entered the house and told Macko she noticed a strange smell in the car, and when Macko walked into the garage to check it out, he arrived just in time to hear a "snap, crackle, pop" and see the car burst into flames. Macko and his wife ran from the house as the fire engulfed the garage and spread throughout both the lower and upper floors. Dozens of firefighters arrived to battle the blaze, and the Mackos watched, from a neighbor's yard, as their home burned to the ground. "You cannot do a thing," Macko said. "That's the sad part about it."

Macko had brought the car in for service at the dealership just days before, so he initially thought the fire had been caused by the new battery the mechanics had installed, but once the fire was out, he got another surprise. He learned he's not the only BMW owner to be left asking questions in the wake of a mysterious fire that started after the car was shut off.

Like many car manufacturers, BMW has issued recalls over the years for fire-related problems, but an ABC-News investigation launched in collaboration with ABC-owned stations in New York, Los Angeles, Chicago, San Francisco, and Raleigh, found more than 40 fires occurring in parked cars across the country in the last five years involving vehicles that did not have open recalls for fire-related issues.

Fire officials in Westchester County, a wealthy enclave outside New York City told WABC-TV they were stunned when they learned how long a 2003 BMW had been sitting parked before it caught on fire.

"The owner told us that the car had been parked for at least four, three or four days," Mamaroneck Fire Chief Tracey Schmaling told WABC investigative reporter Jim Hoffer. "Which we thought was a little peculiar."

According to KABC in Los Angeles, a 2011 BMW parked overnight caught fire last month, damaging the car but sparing the Darth Vader costume its owner Steve Copeland wore in performances at children's charity events. "I had planned to do an event the next day, so Darth Vader's sitting on a mannequin in the front seat, and the police and the fire department thought somebody was in the car when it was on fire, so they busted the windows out," Copeland told KABC. "A couple of the cops thought it was pretty funny. [Darth Vader] has been through a fire before, if you know the story."

And WTVD in Raleigh spoke to Danielle Emerson, a mother of three, who says she was sleeping when her 2011 BMW caught fire in her garage but sprung out of bed to battle the blaze with a garden hose until fire engines arrived. "I need to know what happened," she told WTVD's Diane Wilson. "That could have killed us."

But even as BMW owners and fire departments around the country have raised concerns about these alarming incidents, several BMW owners -- including car club member Macko – told ABC News that BMW gave them the cold shoulder after the fire.

"You're at wit's end, you don't know what to do," Macko said. "I feel like I'm just tossed aside. You know, it's just a number. And so, it's disheartening, I guess, when you're so loyal to a particular product or brand or whatever and then you're treated like this. Not even an apology."

Taz Zaide said that his 2011 BMW 3-series caught on fire about five minutes after he had parked his car to go to work. BMW says it has nothing to apologize for. In a written statement, BMW said that with almost five million BMW vehicles on U.S. roads, such fire incidents are rare, and based on its investigation, "we have not seen any pattern related to quality or component failure. Vehicle fires can result from a wide variety of external reasons unrelated to product defect."

A spokesperson suggested several other potential causes of car fires other than a manufacturing defect, including a lack of maintenance, improper maintenance by unauthorized mechanics, aftermarket modifications, rodent nesting and even arson.

According to auto safety expert Sean Kane, the founder and president of Safety Research & Strategies, the risk of car fires is not an uncommon problem, but they usually occur in cars that are in operation. The mystery of car fires that start after the engine has been turned off, Kane says, may stem from the fact that modern vehicles are never fully powered down.

"A lot of the power to these electronic systems is going to remain on in the vehicle even when the vehicle's off," Kane told ABC News. "And once the electrical system starts going, you've got plenty of combustibles under the hood."

ABC News turned over its findings to the National Highway Traffic Safety Administration, the federal agency charged with enforcing vehicle performance standards. While the agency has not found evidence of a safety defect, they issued a statement directing drivers to their website to "report potential safety issues to the agency, including strange and unexplainable incidents involving their vehicles."

In South Korea, however, the government is taking action. Korean safety officials launched an investigation after a series of car fires involving BMWs--some parked, some not–attracted sustained media attention.

Koh Sungwoo, a South Korean transport ministry official, told ABC News that BMW initially suggested that one of the causes of the fires may have been poor maintenance by unauthorized dealers before acknowledging a fuel line defect affecting some diesel cars. The company issued a recall covering those cars, but the government investigation is still ongoing. Koh said that while poor maintenance and defective fuel lines may explain some of the fires, they do not explain all of them.

"We don't know the exact cause yet. We are still investigating," Koh said. "We have to investigate those incidents because it's very dangerous to the people in Korea."

Brandie Macias told KABC-TV that her 2005 BMW Z4 spontaneously caught fire in the middle of the afternoon while it was parked on the side of the street.

Joseph Santoli, a New Jersey-based attorney who has sued BMW in the past, believes "it's a pattern that BMW is uniquely qualified to remedy," but so far, Santoli told ABC News' Brian Ross, "they have not." Several an-gry BMW owners, Santoli said, have contacted him to explore their legal options.

"I have heard from owners that when they confront BMW about their incident, they're told that this is the first time that BMW has ever heard of it," Santoli told ABC News. "I think some of it is an example of BMW burying their heads in the sand."

The Bavarian Motor Works has offered a discount on a replacement vehicle to some owners; in other cases, the company has paid cash settlements, in which case the company has insisted vehicle owners also sign a non-disclosure agreement. The company says those "goodwill offers" are just "good business to provide support to our loyal customers." BMW insists non-disclosure clauses are executed "to ensure that each incident is evaluated and then appropriately resolved on its own merits," but Santoli believes the true intention of the arrangements is to ensure that the public is less likely to hear about a potential problem.

"That's clearly what they're intending to do," Santoli said. "They're intending to prevent anyone from sharing notes or comparing, or the media finding out." Bill Macko, meanwhile, still isn't sure when he might be able to return home. He and his wife have been staying with relatives while the rebuilding process inches along at what feels to him like a glacial pace.

"I'd like to sleep in my own bed," Macko said in March. "We're working on 15 months, so it would be nice."

Asked if he would ever feel safe enough to park his car in his garage again, Macko said he would. "I'll park my vehicles in there," he said, "but it'll never be a BMW. That won't happen. No. Not at all."

In late 2018 it was announced that BMW is recalling more than 1.4 million cars and SUVs in two U.S. recalls due to the risk of fires under the hood. A spokesman for the German automaker says the risk of fire is very low in both cases, but the vehicles should say outside "in an abundance of caution." In both recalls, repairs are expected to start on Dec. 18, 2018.

The largest of the recalls covers over 740,000 328i, 328xi, 328i xDrive, 525i, 525xi, 528i, 528xi, 530i, 530xi, X3 3.0si, X3 xDrive30i, X5 xDrive30i, Z4 3.0i, Z4 3.0si and Z4 sDrive30i vehicles from 2007-2011. Also included is the 2008-2011 128i. All have 6-Cylinder engines.

Documents posted by the U.S. National Highway Traffic Safety Administration show that a heater for the positive crankcase ventilation valve can overheat and cause the valve to melt, increasing the risk of a fire even when the vehicle is not in use. No injuries have been reported. Dealers will replace the heater. The heater is designed to prevent the valve from freezing in cold temperatures, BMW spokesman Hector Arellano-Belloc said. But irregularities in manufacturing can cause corrosion can lead to overheating.

The other recall covers nearly 673,000 cars including the 323i, 325i, 325xi, 328i, 328xi, 330i, 330xi, 335i, 335xi and M3 from the 2006-2011 model years. Also covered are the 2007-2011 328i xDrive, 335i xDrive and 335is, and the 2009-2011 335d. Wiring for the heating and air conditioning system can overheat and cause connectors to melt, also increasing the fire risk, even when vehicles are unattended. Four drivers reported injuries. BMW says a wiring connection can corrode and in rare cases cause fires. Dealers will replace the wiring and connectors.

Electronic Problems

In German, BMW's Connected Drive slogan is, "Vernetzt um frei zu sein," which translates to "Net-worked, to be free." In 2017, *Motortrend* said, "given the glitchy software in our long-term 530i info-tainment system, it meant something else entirely when I was muttering it under my breath. For starters, anyone with multiple smartphones in their family might be faced with the same problem I found as the BMW rotated through our staff." BMW has multiple problems with electronics, including infotainment and navigation systems.

Motortrend also reported, "any time someone else linked his or her phone to the car, the iDrive system wouldn't recognize my iPhone even though it was still listed as a paired phone (the same thing happened when I upgraded to iOS 11). It often would take upward of an hour to reconnect my phone and get it to work in CarPlay. This is criminal when everyone from Chev-rolet to VW has an almost instant recognition and pairing of smartphones with CarPlay or Android Auto.

Motortrend associate editor Scott Evans had a different, perhaps more obnoxious result: As soon as he got in the BMW, iDrive automatically opened Pandora on his phone even if he had left the car with the stereo set to satellite radio. If you listen to raunchy rap or naughty comedy stations on Pandora, you might want to change over to Chillwave or Sinatra before you take children or clients for a drive in your Bimmer.

Recalls

BMW recalled about 1.4 million vehicles in North America for two separate issues involving risk for fire that results from wiring issues and air conditioning systems. Some vehicles are included in both recalls, BMW said. However, considering that BMW only produces 2.5 mil-lion cars a year, a recall of this magnitude is daunting.

Specifically, one recall involves 670,000 2006-2011

model years 323i, 325i, 325xi, 328i, 328xi, 330i, 330xi, 335i, 335xi and M3. Also covered are the 2007-2011 328i xDrive, 335i xDrive and 335is, and the 2009-2011 335d that have a risk of fire that results from air conditioning systems that may overheat.

BMW reported to the National Highway Traffic Safety Administration about the heating and air conditioning issues following its first report of an incident in 2008 involving heat-related damage to a 2006 3-Series sedan. However, BMW did not determine a root cause, but did continue to monitor incident reports.

BMW made a quality improvement to the blower-regulator wiring harness in 2011. While there were no re-ports of injuries between 2007 and 2014, in 2015, BMW was made aware of three incidents in which there were allegations of injuries. In early September, 2015, BMW learned of another incident involving a 2011 BMW 3 Series vehicle.

The second recall involves 740,000 US vehicles with a valve heater that could rust and result in fire. The recall includes some 328i, 328xi, 328i xDrive, 525i, 525xi, 528i, 528xi, 530i, 530xi, X3 3.0si, X3 xDrive30i, X5 xDrive30i, Z4 3.0i, Z4 3.0si and Z4 sDrive30i vehicles from 2007-2011. Also included is the 2008-2011 128i.

All have six-cylinder engines.

Regarding the second recall, BMW received its first report in 2009, involving an incident in a 2007 X5 with heat-related damage to the engine compartment, the company told NHTSA. It received other reports and continued to review the issue and inspect returned parts, but had no reports of injuries or crashes related to the issue, according to Reuters.com.

BMW spokesman Michael Rebstock said the recalls overlap and cover about one million vehicles, nearly all in the United States and about 15,000 in Canada. He said the recalls may be expanded, *Reuters* reports.

Faulty Fuel Pump Recall

BMW had another recall that involved defective wiring. BMW recalled certain model year 2007-2011 BMW X5 3.0si, X5 4.8i, X5 M, X5 xDrive30i, X5 xDrive35i, X5 xDrive48i and X5 xDrive50i, 2008-2011 X6 x Drive35i, X6 xDrive50i and X6 M, 2010-2011 X6 ActiveHybrid, 535i xDrive Gran Turismo, 535i Gran Turismo, 550i xDrive Gran Turismo and 550i Gran Turismo, 2011-2012 528i, 535i, 535i xDrive, 550i and 550i xDrive and 2012 535i ActiveHybrid, 640i Convertible, 650i Convertible, 650i xDrive Convertible, 650i Coupe and

650i Coupe xDrive vehicles. The affected vehicles have in-tank fuel pumps that may have insufficiently crimped wire contacts.

The loose wires may cause the connector to melt, resulting in a fuel leak. Additionally, the fuel pump may stop working, possibly causing an engine stall and increase the risk of a crash. 136,188 vehicles are affected by the recall

BMW will notify owners, and dealers will replace the fuel pump module, free of charge. The recall began December of 2016.

(DWA) Drinking While Assembling BMWs

Bavaria is known primarily for two things: BMW (Bavarian Motor Works) and beer drinking. The two don't mix well. BMW has beer vending machines in every break room

At a BMW plant in Munich, Germany, production came to a standstill for almost an hour after two workers had passed out during their shift due to alcohol and drug consumption.

Confirming a report in the German tabloid *Bild*, the Munich-based premium carmaker said two of its assembly line workers had collapsed towards the end of their shift earlier this month after drinking "copious amounts of alcohol" and smoking synthetic marijuana. Other BMW employees had called for an ambulance, which caused production to be suspended for a period of 40 minutes, a BMW spokesman said.

The mass-circulation *Bild* reported that one of the workers had been fired and the other moved to a different location. The story refers to an incident that was con-firmed to have taken place on March 3, 2017, when two employees from one of its assembly lines collapsed near the end of their shifts.

One of the workers was fired, while the other was relocated to a different location. BMW has not named them, but reports noted that one of them had amphetamines in his bloodstream, while the other was just flat-out drunk. It is believed that the former was fired for getting high on the job, while the other was moved to a different facility.

The delay in output was initially evaluated at over a million euros, but BMW specified that the losses fell "in the five-figure range." That means that hundreds of thousands of euros were lost by the company because two guys got drunk and high on their break. The two workers were on the third shift of the plant, which operates late into the night. According to reports, they fell unconscious around 10:40 p.m.

Class Actions Against BMW

Every car company has been sued in class actions. However, BMW has been sued more than most. In addition it has paid very large settlements (not as large as Volkswagen's diesel class action settlement.)

On October 18, 2016, a federal judge ruled that a class action lawsuit against BMW that claims the engine in the M3 performance model is defective can proceed to trial. The complaint also asserts that BMW knew of the defect and failed to disclose it to prospective or current owners. The BMW complaint states that the S65 engine in 2008 to 2013 model BMW M3 vehicles has a defective rotating assembly. Allegedly, the defect creates an "insufficient supply of engine oil to coat the bearing surfaces" of the connecting rod bearings, which causes "accelerated wear on the Bearings surfaces in all BMW M3s, ultimately causing them to disintegrate and fracture." The lawsuit alleges this defect creates a "rattling" or "clacking" noise when the engine is idling.

The bearing defect can lead to "catastrophic engine failure," according to the BMW M3 class action lawsuit. As the metal bearings wear down, pieces of bearing metal get distributed throughout the engine in the engine oil. The complaint alleges that this can lead to many different serious issues, such as a loss of power steering, or power assistance to the braking system.

The BMW lawsuit claims that not only does the defect create a safety hazard, it also diminishes the value of the BMW M3, particularly its resale value. Plaintiff David Afzal states that he purchased a 2011 BMW M3 in 2013 from a BMW dealership after receiving a vehicle inspection from the dealership. In March of 2015, while the vehicle was still under warranty, Afzal allegedly heard a knocking sound from the car and took it into the dealership. The dealership stated, twice, that it was "normal exhaust noise," according to the class action lawsuit. Afzal asserts that an independent repair facility diagnosed that the bearing rods needed to be replaced, at a cost of over $2,000.

The BMW M3 class action lawsuit seeks to create a Class of all U.S. residents who are current owners, former owners, or people who have leased a 2011-2015 model BMW M3. The class action lawsuit seeks damages for each member of the Class, and to require BMW to repair or replace the defective engines through a recall or extension of its warranty. *Afzal v. BMW of North Am-erica LLC,* et al., Case No. 2:15-CV-08009, in the U.S. District Court for the District of New Jersey, Newark Di-vision.

Eight-Cylinder Case

Another class action lawsuit was against BMW claiming defects in the N63 eight-cylinder engine. According to plaintiff Scott Crockett, the N63 engine has serious defects including excessive burning of oil and battery consumption. He further alleges that BMW has taken insufficient measures in an attempt to re-mediate the problem, by attempting to cover it up rather than deal with it directly.

A visit to any online BMW enthusiast community will quickly show what members think of the N63 engine. The same complaints raised by the plaintiff in the class action lawsuit are mentioned there, much to the disappointment of the brand's performance car enthusiasts. Compared to similar vehicles with other engines, those with the N63 engines appear to continually disappoint.

Apparently, BMW is aware of the shortcomings brought forth in the class action lawsuit, as they have allegedly issued service bulletins to BMW service technicians performing warranty-covered maintenance under BMW's Standard Maintenance Program. One bulletin states, "However, in a quest to ensure total customer satisfaction, please replace the 12-volt battery on a preventive maintenance basis at every engine oil service ... unless the battery was replaced within the last 12 months."

Another service bulletin allegedly instructs technicians to add double the oil that was originally recommended. According to the BMW class action lawsuit, these remedies are simply being used to mask the engine defect, possibly until the 48-month or 50,000-mile warranty has expired.

In addition to the service bulletins issued for known engine defects, the BMW class action lawsuit maintains that the "N63 Customer Care Package" is another way to hide the problems without addressing them directly. This care package offered customers additional inspection and replacement of other engine parts, even beyond the initial warranty. It also reduced the amount of time between services, from the initial 2-year interval to a yearly oil change. The "N63 Customer Loyalty Offer" provided customers with discounts if they were unhappy with their vehicle and wished to replace it. Lastly, the customer care package allowed dealerships to provide those who purchased the vehicle up to $50 in BMW merchandise and/or accessories.

In what some purchasers have dubbed a lemon, vehicles with the N63 engine also apparently suffer from diminished resale value. When resale buyers are looking at reviews on potential purchases, the BMWs with the N63 engine are a hard sell. Four claims are brought against BMW in the class action lawsuit: violation of the Manguson-Moss Warranty Act, breach of express war-ranty, breach of implied warranty of merchantability and violation of the Kansas Consumer Protection Act. *Crock-ett v. BMW of North America LLC,* Case No. 2:15-cv-09266, in the U.S. District Court for the District of Kansas.

TwinPower Turbo Lawsuit

BMW was hit with a class action lawsuit accusing the company of deceiving consumers by marketing vehicles as "TwinPower Turbo" engines when they are allegedly only single-turbocharger engines.

Lead plaintiff, California resident Deepkarn Singh Bedi claims that in late 2012 he researched and decided to lease a new BMW 335i. According to the lawsuit, the dealership's advertising as well as information on the internet indicated that the car had "TwinPower Turbo" engines, which the plaintiff thought were the more powerful Twin Turbo engines. Bedi claims he later discovered that BMW uses the term "TwinPower Turbo" for both actual twin turbo engines and single turbo engines interchangeably.

"Twin-turbo engines are objectively superior to single-turbo engines," the lawsuit alleges. "Conventional driving tests can measure this superior performance. For ex-ample, twin-turbo engines boast reduced turbo lag, superior throttle response, smoother delivery of power and torque, and greater ease of tuning."

"Because a twin-turbo engine is significantly better than a single-turbo engine, twin-turbo engines are particularly prestigious and sought after, thereby commanding a price premium relative to non-twin-turbo vehicles," the BMW class action lawsuit continues. "BMW's actions demonstrate the importance of twin-turbocharging in establishing brand prestige and performance, so as to com-mand a price premium. Had it been otherwise, BMW would have more routinely employed single-turbo engines in place of the twin turbos."

According to the complaint, BMW began using the term "TwinPower Turbo" to market its less powerful models that relied on twin scrolling. "In developing the single-turbo N55 engine to replace the twin-turbo N54, BMW faced a marketing problem stemming from the loss of a turbo, and a deviation from the proud heritage of the N54," Bedi alleges. "Because the N55 might be perceived as a downgrade from the N54 (going from a twin turbo to a single turbo), BMW described the False Twin N55 engine, and vehicles with the same, as 'TwinPower Turbo.' In doing so, BMW relied on the cachet associated with the twin-turbo N54."

Both the plaintiff and other BMW purchasers believed the term "TwinPower Turbo" meant the vehicles they purchased contained the more powerful twin turbo engine, rather than the single turbo engine, according to the BMW class action lawsuit. The BMW models that contain single turbo engines but are referenced as "TwinPower Turbo" include all N55 and N20 variants manufactured from 2012 until the present. *Bedi v.*

BMW of North America LLC, Case No. 2:15-cv-01898, in U.S. District Court for the District of New Jersey.

Navigation Lawsuit Settled

Karen Morris filed a class action lawsuit against BMW in 2013 alleging that the navigation system which she opted to add-on to her 2012 BMW 5 series vehicle for $1,800 was faulty. According to Morris, the navigation system did not give the right directions, it resets without warning, and does not properly identify locations. In addition, she alleges that BMW knew of the problems with navigation system based on the automaker's own tests and tests performed by third parties as well as complaints from customers and reports from local dealerships.

When she asked for a refund for the $1,800 she spent on the system, BMW told her that the problem wasn't with the navigation system itself but with the map.

Karen Morris et al. v. BMW of North America LLC ,Case No. 2:13-cv-04980, in the U.S. District Court for the District of New Jersey. The case was settled and BMW owners with navigation problems can receive compensation or a new nav system.

Remote Locking Lawsuit

BMW was hit with a class action lawsuit claiming that the luxury car manufacturer's hands-free remote locking feature used to lock and unlock doors is defective. According to the claim, certain vehicles have spontaneously locked, without driver input, locking keys and sometimes children inside the vehicle.

Plaintiff Kieva Myers filed the class action lawsuit in California federal court, stating that all BMW X5 vehicles manufactured from model year 2008 to 2015 were equipped with a remote locking system that is potentially defective, causing car doors to sometimes lock auto-matically, potentially trapping keys and young children inside.

The BMW X5 manual for Myers' 2013 vehicle states that the "comfort feature" of automatically locking doors allows the vehicle to be accessed without the driver actually having to touch the remote control, according to the complaint. The BMW class action lawsuit further explains that the doors can be locked or unlocked by simply detecting that the remote control is in range, say, in the driver's purse or pocket, and the feature is activated.

However, when the remote key is inside of the vehicle the feature is supposed to be disabled so the keys are not inadvertently locked inside of the car, but Myers claims this isn't the case.

Myers says she put her child in the vehicle, placed her remote in the vehicle and shut the door. As she attempted to open the driver side door, it had already locked on its own spontaneously, according to the lawsuit. Myers' child was locked in the car and was too young to be able to open the car from the inside.

Myers said she had to break the vehicle's window to get her daughter out, damaging her vehicle and terrifying her child in the process. Myers contacted BMW directly to make a complaint about the alleged defective remote locking feature. In an email back to Myers, a representative responded, "Therefore, we must be dealing either with a malfunction of the locking system or an inadvertent activation of the locking system via either the remote transmitter or the Comfort Access System. Again – it is not impossible to lock a key in the vehicle- and to do so is not necessarily indicative of a malfunction."

Myers claimed that BMW's response to her complaint was a complete contradiction to her owner's manual that stated, "To lock the vehicle, the remote control must be located outside of the vehicle." Myers asserts that the manual is false and misleading, saying, "Class vehicles locking by themselves is extremely unsafe."

Three other consumers complained to the National Highway Traffic and Safety Administration about the remote locking feature spontaneously locking. Two of the instances involved keys being locked in the car and the third was a similar situation to Myers' where police and firemen were called to the vehicle and had to smash a window to get the driver's child out who was locked in the car.

Myers hopes to represent a nationwide class of BMW X5 owners and lessees and a California subclass as well. She is seeking reimbursement for the cost to repair her car, as well as compensatory, exemplary and statutory damages.

Myers v. BMW of North America LLC, Case No. 3:16-cv-00412, U.S. District Court for the Northern District of California.

Defective Sunroofs

BMW has settled two class-action lawsuits that claimed the manufacturer's sunroofs were defective on certain makes and models, resulting in thousands of dollars' worth of damage not covered under warranty. The lawsuit, which was brought by California residents Monita Sharma and Eric Anderson in 2013, states that certain vehicles' sunroof drain tubes get clogged, allowing water to enter the area of the spare tire and cause damage to important electrical components. The result was $2,000 worth of damage that Anderson had to cover himself, as a dealer informed him it wasn't covered by warranty.

The vehicles listed in the settlement include 2004-2010 BMW 5 Series (E60 and E61), and states that these models aren't protected from potential water damage, which could ruin electrical components that are expensive to have fixed or replaced.

The original complaint states, "BMW designed, manufactured, distributed, sold, and leased various makes and models of BMW vehicles that contain a serious design defect that significantly impacts both the safety and value of its vehicles. Specifically, numerous models of BMW vehicles manufactured during the class period were designed so that certain vital electrical components known as SDARS, RDC, and PDC modules, are located in the lowest part of the vehicles' trunk. …. Because BMW decided to place these vital electrical components in what is essentially the lowest part of the vehicle (the spare tire well under the trunk), they are especially prone to water damage that can be caused through the normal and ordinary use of the vehicle."

When this water damage occurs, the vehicles become inoperable and pose a serious safety risk to those who experience this problem. Although these components are highly susceptible to water damage, BMW provides no warnings or advisories to BMW owners about the location of this vital equipment or the importance of keeping the vehicle's trunk compartment free of liquids," the lawsuit continued. BMW did not confess to any wrongdoing or negligence but moved forward with a settlement to avoid the added cost and time of a continued trial.

According to the settlement, BMW owners of affected vehicles can schedule an appointment with an authorized BMW dealer for an inspection within one year of the final settlement date. Any water-damaged components will be repaired or replaced. In addition, any owner who paid out-of-pocket to cover repair or replacement expenses will be reimbursed, up to $1,500, after submitting a claim and providing evidence of the repair. Dealers will also affix a warning label to the trunks of vehicles.

Defective Subframes

A class action lawsuit against BMW was filed federal court in Los Angeles, California alleging that 1999-2006 BMW 3 series vehicles suffer from defective sub-frames. The suit claimed that BMW was aware of the alleged defect, but failed to notify consumers or pay for sub-frame repairs under warranty. The lawsuit additionally alleged consumer fraud, deceptive advertising, and that BMW had implemented a secret warranty program.

The case was settled. Under the settlement, class members nationwide received full reimbursement for prior sub-frame repair costs as well as free inspections and, if needed, repairs to their sub-frames.

Convertible Case Settled

A nationwide settlement has been reached in a class action lawsuit against BMW regarding defective convertible tops on the BMW 6 Series. The lawsuit claimed that the convertible top would not completely open or close, becomes stuck in a fixed position, the convertible top operation light flashes, causing the "top not locked" warning message to appear, and/or causes an alarm to sound. The Settlement provides an opportunity to be reimbursed for certain past expenses and to obtain a free software update to remedy the issue.

BMWi3 Lawsuit

MLG Automotive Law filed a national class action lawsuit against BMW for alleged defects in the BMW i3 vehicles. The lawsuit centers around the BMW i3 "Range Extender" feature. This option, called REx, outfits the vehicle with a two-cylinder gasoline engine producing 34 horsepower that switches on when the battery charge depletes to five percent, giving the vehicle another 70 miles of range. BMW claims that the Range Extender "doubles your electric driving range" from the vehicle's standard 81-mile range.

The lawsuit claims that in practice, however, when the gasoline engine kicks in, it doesn't produce enough power to prevent a dramatic decrease in the vehicle's performance. If the car is under any kind of significant load (such as going up a hill, or loaded with passengers), the speed of the car will dramatically decrease as the battery charge diminishes. The lawsuit alleges that this can result in the car slowing to speeds of 45 miles per hour on the freeway, without warning.

"The BMW i3 Range Extender feature is a dangerous instrumentality to the owners of the vehicles and to other motorists on the road," said Jonathan Michaels, founding member of MLG Automotive Law. "Having a sudden and unexpected loss of power in a motor vehicle can result in a catastrophic situation for all those on the road. These cars are dangerous and should not be driven."

The lawsuit seeks to have the vehicles redesigned and repaired at BMW's expense, and to halt the sale of all i3 vehicles until repairs can be made. The claim also seeks compensation for all the owners of the vehicles, who were not told of the serious safety defect. *Edo Tsoar v. BMW North America, LLC* (Case No. 2:16-cv-03386) U.S. Dis-trict Court in Los Angeles.

A Woman's Viewpoint

Meg Amor, a professional writer, often writes about cars. She is a BMW aficionado:

> I've owned three BMWs. All V8s. One new 540, two secondhand, a 540 and a 535. But when they do have to go in for repair. Ouch. If I came out with an under

thousand-dollar repair, I thought that was quite good. There are some standard things that always seem to go in Beemers.

I blew the radiator in all three of mine. Standard Beemer thing. And cooked the thermostat housing and wiring. It took my mechanic four hours to finally do this when he rung me to ask: Do you have another key for this, she won't turn over, after I'd had her towed in.

Check the fuses, it's a Beemer, I said. Aha, aha, he said. Four hours later he called back - I'm going to listen to you next time. The fuses, yes? I said.

My dad taught my sister and I to listen for noises and things that sound off in an engine. So I do go and investigate what I think might be going on with my car before I take it anywhere.

My 535 was a horrible car and I used to go on there a lot to figure out what was going on...now.

The sensors for various things seem to crap out unexpectedly. I had the AC sensor go in one, an engine sensor in another. Lots in my 535 which hadn't been looked after.

Beemers can often have 'quirky' things go wrong with them."

Oil Burners

Consumer Reports conducted a study of half a million cars where consumers complained of excessive oil use. The leading consumer magazine found that BMW's 4.8-liter V8 and twin-turbocharged 4.4-liter V8 were excessive burners of engine oil. The worst case showed that, overall, owners of BMW 5 Series vehicles with V8 engines were 27 times as likely to suffer excessive oil consumption as owners of an average vehicle.

BMW responded that oil consumption is a normal part of a car's operation. Certain BMW cars' standards state that a quart burned every 600 to 700 miles is reasonable.

If a driver has to add a quart of oil once per month, that can mean adding up to 7 to 9 quarts of oil between oil changes. Those costs due to excessive oil consumption can add up because automakers more frequently require synthetic oils that can cost upwards of $9 per quart—in addition to the expense of the routine oil changes.

Consumer Reports data does not show a direct connection between increased oil consumption and other engine problems. But CU's survey data concerning 10 model years shows that if a car burns oil early in its life, it will burn even more as it ages. In tracking oil consumption by model year, engine families show increased consumption with each successive year on the road. *Consumer Reports* believes that any engine that burns oil between changes should be repaired under the power-train warranty.

Putting on the Weight

Fugly: Fat and ugly, that is what is happening to BMW. The Wall Street Journal's car guy, Dan Neil, calls BMW's latest SUV, "garish, overweight, and underwhelming X7 sport-utility vehicle." Neil continues, "My problem is with the outside. It's a bag of doorknobs. May I draw your attention to the section between the front-axle centerline and steering wheel, including cowl, windshield and front roof pillars. This area represents the least flexible part of BMW's new rear-drive vehicle platform, called Cluster Architecture, or CLAR, which the X7 shares with the also-new 7 Series sedan. For whatever reason, the X7's design-engineering team kept the sedan's landmarks largely in place."

Mr. Neil opines:

> As a result, the front third of the X7 has a sedan's anatomy, the long hood and front overhang, only a foot higher. Filling in the difference produced the visual massiveness in the X7's nose. The hood line is so long it actually flattens out before rising again at the base of the windshield (the scuttle). That is something a hood line should never do.
>
> Observe how the side sill line, the bottom edge of the windows, starts well below the base of the windshield (the scuttle). That's fine for a minivan, but in an SUV the visual expectation is for those lines to meet—to trade off, sky and glass, at the scuttle. Seen in profile, the misalignment creates the impression of a fault line

between the main masses of the vehicle. The front doors' hollowed cheeks and the spars of brightwork behind the front-wheel arches help de-emphasize, but do not fully conceal, the rift.

Item last on my ugly list: the lower front clip of our X7 xDrive 50i, the triptych of openings below the chrome nostrils, filled with black plastic grillework, active louvers *behind* grillework, and the active-safety system's radar sensor, mounted its own parentheses-shaped inset. The left lateral intake in blocked off, and non-functional. But it's so big you can't help noting the fakery. In a vehicle costing $117,945 that's pretty galling.

I did also accuse the X7 of being overweight and underwhelming. At 5,617 pounds, the X7 xDrive50i might be the heaviest vehicle BMW has ever made, unless it built some Ultimate Driving Forklifts I never heard of.

Conclusion

BMWs aren't what they used to be. This may be because BMW is making too many different models and too many types of vehicles. It may also be that BMW has not kept up with technological advances in electronics. Further, BMWs have become much more complicated than twenty or thirty years ago. In addition, repairs to BMWs are very expensive, making it the world's most expensive vehicle to maintain. While BMWs have excellent performance, their reliability and flammability is extremely suspect.

Chapter Five

Death by Porsche: The Most Dangerous Cars on the Planet

"The Porsche Carrera GT is the first car in my life that I drive and I feel scared"–

Senior Porsche Test Driver Walter Röhrl

In June 1934, Ferdinand Porsche received a contract from Hitler to design a "people's car" (*Volkswagen*). This resulted in the Volkswagen Beetle. Dan Neil, the Wall Street Journal's automotive writer said, "Ferdinand Porsche was an enthusiastic National Socialist party member and Hitler's car guy. Attempts to portray the founder of Porsche as a reluctant Nazi are misguided and unsupported by the evidence.

Among other crimes, Porsche directed wartime production in factories using forced labor and guarded by units of the SS. Porsche himself was awarded the rank of SS-Oberführer. So let us, as lovers of automobiles and history, not kid ourselves about who Porsche was . . . ."

The first models of what was to become the Porsche 356 were produced in 1948. Like the Beetle, it had the engine in the rear. Many have called it a high-performance Beetle. The Porsche 550, an updated version of the 356, was a racing sports car produced by Porsche from 1953- 1956. Hollywood film legend James Dean died—young and badly, crashing his Porsche 550 on September 30, 1955. In 1964, after a fair amount of success in motor-racing with various models including the 550 Spyder, the company launched the Porsche 911: another air-cool-ed, rear-engined sports car, this time with a six-cylinder "boxer" engine.

After a half century in production, the Porsche 911 is generally considered to be one of the most iconic sports cars in the world. But to paraphrase the old cliché, Porsche took a bad idea and refined it to brilliance. Not only is the 911's engine in the back of the car, it's so far behind the rear axle that even the slightest miscalculation could cause dangerous oversteer, sending you hurtling backwards into oncoming traffic.

Porsche engineers first tried to solve the car's weight imbalance by putting iron weights in the front bumpers of early cars. By the early 1970s, the 911's iconic "whale tail" spoiler and front air dam did the trick to keep the car planted to the ground at speed. Today, an all-wheel drive system and traction control have overcome out most of the 911's homicidal urges, but the older cars are undeniably deathly.

Hanging a massive lump of metal (the engine) out past the rear axle increases the car's polar moment of inertia, which makes it harder to regain control once the car begins a slide. This was the basic problem with the Corvair that Ralph Nader ridiculed in *Unsafe at Any Speed,* but the Corvair had a smaller, lighter engine.

This isn't a real problem for a 40 horsepower VW Beetle with a small engine hanging beyond the rear axle, but as power and speeds increase, it becomes a serious problem. We could discuss physics at length, but since the vast majority of modern racecars are equipped with an engine mounted amidship, the 911's layout remains a dangerous outlier.

As many as 200 of the 1,200 Carrera GTs which Porsche produced have been totaled in the first two years it was sold (2004-2006), one Porsche employee wrote in an email exchange about a body shop employee who had just wrecked another example of the supercar. The email continued with, "Another Carrera GT bites the dust. Looks like he was going more than 30 (mph) to me!"

Jonathan Mills, an auto writer for Petrolicious.com, wrote,

> As you might well know, the 911 is a marvel of engineering that goes very, very fast and then tries to kill you when you turn. This is due directly to the dynamic issues inherent to having a six-cylinder engine hanging off the back of the car and as a result, when I hit the first curve the car was willing ... I wasn't.
>
> There was a little dip, a dip you wouldn't notice at normal speeds, however, I wasn't traveling at normal speeds and as a result just as I initiated

my left turn the rear went light and just like that I was spinning, across Wilshire (major thoroughfare in Los Angeles), in midday traffic.

Porsche has tried for decades to counter the properties of basic physics that make Porsche's so dangerous. One is the Porsche Stability Management (PSM) system, an electronic safety device that was intentionally left off the Carrera GT, which the German automaker marketed as a "*supercar that can be driven every day." Porsche enthusiasts jokingly refer to PSM as "Please Save Me."

In 2006, the National Highway Traffic Safety Administration ruled that stability control systems must be included in all cars sold in the USA by 2012. The feature, the name of which varies by manufacturer, uses electronic sensors linked to the braking system to slow the car and help the driver maintain control when traveling at speed, cornering or across slippery surfaces. That year, the Insurance Institute for Highway Safety estimated that it could prevent "nearly one-third of all fatal crashes and reduce rollover risk by as much as 80%."

After acknowledging the "high-profile deaths and lawsuits" involving the Carrera GT, auto journalist Doug DeMuro noted in a 2015 video profile, "No automaker with any sort of reasonable, decent legal department will ever go near anything like this again."

Porsche Turbo

Frank Markus of *Car and Driver* wrote: "911 Turbos were always prone to sudden oversteer when their afterburner-like turbo boost kicked in. And now there's more power? It's clear corporate negligence and irresponsibility. Tens of innocent people will surely spin, crash, and burn at the helm of this deathtrap." Markus wrote that Porsche could not overcome the laws of physics: "all the engine, tire, and suspension innovations can't change the laws of physics. And if you just plain enter a curve too fast and jump off the throttle, you're still likely to pirouette into the poppies."

Death by Battery

A mother and her three-year old daughter were found dead in a 2006 Porsche Cayenne on Florida's Turnpike in 2016. Latifa Lincoln, 45, and her daughter, Maksmilla Lincoln, were found dead inside the SUV. A strong odor forced first responders back. Three of them reported breathing problems. Investigators have since determined the mother and daughter did not die as the result of a crime or auto accident.

After months of intensive investigation on the vehicle at the medical examiner's office in Orlando, Assistant Medical Examiner Dr. Gary Utz said he found that the mother and daughter died of hydrogen sulfide intoxication, as the result of a defect in the car's battery.

"It's unprecedented," Utz said. "I haven't been able to find another case." Utz said he found elevated levels of hydrogen sulfide in the victim's urine. He sent the battery to the National Highway Traffic Safety Administration in to have more tests done. He's also sent "darkened coins" found in the SUV to an Ohio lab in hopes of determining the substance on them is hydrogen sulfide. The clear, flammable gas can smell like rotten eggs. Hydrogen sulfide in high concentrations can cause sudden death.

Unlike many vehicles that have the battery under the hood, the Porsche Cayenne battery is found under the driver's seat. Vehicle identification records confirm Lincoln bought the car in May from an East Orlando dealership. A manager at Auto Express on Goldenrod Road confirmed they sold the SUV to Lincoln.

"We feel sorry for the lady," said finance manager Ron Telleysh. "She used to come in here all the time with her little daughter." He said the vehicle had never been in-volved in a crash. The only work they did on the SUV was some upholstery repairs to the back of the vehicle's passenger seat. Orlando television station WESH confirmed through vehicle identification records there is no crash noted in the vehicle's history.

Failure to consider the deadly consequences of installing a battery in the passenger compartment of an SUV dem-onstrates the German engineering failed to protect human passengers. The reason the battery was placed under the driver's seat was probably for weight balance to improve performance. The engineers involved should weigh health and safety concerns above performance.

Porsche Death Rattle

Autologic published the following warning to Porsche owners:

> If you are a 1997 to 2008 Porsche owner by now you've heard stories of the fabled Porsche death rattle. An engine failure

related to Intermediate Shaft Bearing (IMS) that has plagued close to 10% of the following Porsche vehicles:

- 911 Models 1997 to 2008
- All Boxster Models 1997-2008
- All Cayman Models 2006-2008

The intermediate shift bearing failure is characterized by an ominous engine rattle that occurs when the bearings begin to fail and come apart. Once heard, the end of the engine is near and the start of a costly rebuild process begins, and in some cases are not covered by the warranty. But it can be stopped. By paying careful attention for any leak at the IMS hub flange (which in many cases can be improperly identified as a rear main seal (RMS) leak), and noticing early signs of a failing bearing, then replacing it before it breaks apart. Since not all engines have had this problem it is not recommended to do an IMS retrofit immediately, instead paying careful attention to the IMS hub flange at short intervals when nearing the 30,000 mile mark on the odometer. An IMS change can also be done at the same time as an RMS leak repair as the majority of the labor is identical to that of performing the RMS service.

There are retrofit kits designed for all Porsche models. These replacement retrofits replace faulty sealed bearings with a heavy-duty ceramic roller ball bearing for a more reliable performance under higher temperatures and are in used in place of the factory IMS flange hub, bearing support, and fastener with a stronger, revised billet chromoly assembly.

Not all Porsche engines have had this problem. However, once the death rattle is heard there is little that can be done to save the engine.

Apparently, Porsche is also having trouble with the engines in certain SUVs. According to the National High-way Traffic Safety Administration, some of those vehicles "have camshaft controllers that may come loose inside the engine, potentially resulting in an engine stall."

Since a stalling engine wouldn't come as very good news for most Porsche owners, the company is recalling in 17,986 of them in the United States alone. Included among them are Panameras – including base, S, 4, 4S, and Turbo models – from the 2010-12 model years, and certain 2011 Cayenne S and Cayenne Turbo SUVs as well.

Porsche Recalls

The National Highway Traffic Safety Administration has forced several recalls of Porsches. made by the luxury automaker and reported by the National Highway Traffic Safety Administration. NHTSA recall included covered 288 vehicle Porsches from the years 2013-'14. Of these, 207 Cayenne models were being called back due to a fuel gauge problem. The 2014 cars included in the action were the Boxster, Cayman and Carerra models suffering from airbag problems.

Porsche was recalling the 2013 Cayenne Diesel, 2013-14 Cayenne and Cayenne GTS and 2014 models including the Cayenne S, Turbo, S Hybrid, and Turbo S due to an inaccurate fuel gauge. The problem could lead to the cars running out of gas before the gauge showed the tank was empty. The concern was that the car could then stall out in traffic, leading to an accident, the NHTSA said.

The airbag problem in the 81 recalled 2014 cars could cause the devices meant for the passenger front seat and knee areas to become deactivated, the safety agency said, adding that defective wiring harnesses could cause the airbags not to deploy in an accident, thereby increasing the injury risk to a passenger in the front seat.

Although a car crash can be caused by faulty auto parts, often catastrophic injuries are caused due to a distracted driver like one who is texting and driving. Sometimes a car accident can occur due to a drunk driver taking the wheel despite all the laws against it. An auto accident can also be caused by a reckless driver going too fast for conditions. Whatever the cause, a car accident attorney may be able to help a victim to seek compensation in a court of law.

Porsche Pyrotechnics

Like its cousin the BMW, Porsche has also had an unusual share of car fires. Porsche is telling owners to stop driving one of its high-performance models after two of the cars caught fire. The notice affects 785 model-year 2014 Porsche 911 GT3s. There are 408 of the cars in the United States. The GT3 is a sporty two-seat version of the 911 that is often used for racing. Prices for this model starts at $130,000. The 911 GT3 can go from zero to 60 miles per hour in just 3.3 seconds, with a top speed of 195 miles per hour.

Porsche said engine damage occurred in two vehicles that caught fire in Europe. The company is still investigating the fires. The automaker is contacting the owners of the 911 GT3s directly and offering to pick up the vehicles so that it can inspect the engines at a dealership. In a statement, The National Highway Traffic Safety Administration said it is in contact with Porsche and "aware of proactive steps taken by the automaker to ensure the safety of its customers."

Porsche will replace the engines in 785 high-performance sports cars because of a risk that the current engines could catch fire. The move was made in response to two engine fires in Porsche 911 GT3s. The decision to replace the engines was made after Porsche engineers investigated two engine fires that occurred in Europe. Engineers discovered that the fires were caused by a loose rod inside the engine. The loose rod caused damage that then allowed lubricating oil to leak out and ignite.

About 135,000 Porsche and Volkswagen sport utilities were recalled over the danger of a fuel leak, according to documents from the automakers posted on the website of the National Highway Traffic Safety Administration. In its report, Porsche said the action covers about 50,000 vehicles. They include the Porsche 2004-06 Cayenne, 2003-06 Cayenne S and 2003-06 Cayenne Turbo. Volkswagen told federal regulators about 74,000 2004-07 Touareg models are covered.

The automakers' reports did not mention whether there were any fires. The recalls come about a year after Audi recalled about 143,000 corporate siblings, the 2009-12 Q5 and 2007-12 Q7 for the same problem. That problem is that "fine hairline cracks can appear, after an extended period of use, on the filter flange of the fuel pump," the automaker said. That would allow "a very small quantity" of fuel to leak.

What was supposed to be a date to discuss wedding details quickly went up in in smoke for an East Memphis woman after her Porsche Boxter caught fire. "We were actually going to meet our wedding planner for the first time," said Kim-An Hernandez. "I made quite the impression on her." Hernandez shared how her 2017 Porsche 718 Boxster went up in flames on May 13th. "It was just frightening," she said. "I pulled the emergency brake and jumped out of the car and it was just smoke and smoke and smoke. Fire was just coming out from underneath it."

According to Hernandez, her brand new, $80,000 Boxster had about 5,000 miles on the odometer. "I didn't get a chance to do that road trip where you put the top down," she said. "I just never got to experience that." Instead, she found herself calling 911 and running into Muddy's Bake Shop for fire extinguishers.

Hernandez is speaking out after she learned the automaker had several recalls on Boxster models, although her vehicle was specifically listed. "At no point was I ever made aware of what I now know is rampant fire concerns around a whole host of their vehicles," she said.

According to National Highway Traffic Safety Administration there have been several recall campaigns on the 2017 Porsche 718 Boxter. According to the recall data-base one of those campaigns covers more than 4,000 unites of that model Boxster.

The campaign sites a "fuel leak due to sheared fastening screws." Those screws pose a fire risk. "I could have been killed," said Hernandez. "What if this happened when I was on the highway? What if other people around me were hurt?"

Porsche fires are not uncommon, as Porsche leads the world in cars on fire. The Nashville Fire Department released four 911 calls made to Metro Nashville Fire & Police's emergency dispatch center around 1:30 p.m. September 22, 2017. The calls reported that a Porsche was on fire at the intersection of Lafayette Street and 4th Avenue, just off Interstate 40. "It looked like a convertible," one of the callers said. "The man is out of the car and motioning people to get to the other side of the road."

Another caller identified herself as Hazel Berger, the niece of the driver. After reaching Berger on the phone via call and text, she offered to share our contact information with her uncle, whom she declined to iden-tify. Nashville Fire Department Public Information Of-ficer Joseph Pleasant identified the vehicle's owner as Ann Bodnar of Franklin, Tennessee. Both fire and police sources said the 911 calls are the only records of the fire. No one wrote an incident report identifying the model of the Porsche.

The Unique Porsche Smell

Stan Hanks, an auto writer for *Quora*, fell in love with Porsche in 1971. Stan was asked about the distinctive Porsche smell. He responded, "If you're talking about a 911 or really any of the flat-engine cars, it's burning oil. The air-cooled cars are particularly bad about this - they are actually oil cooled, and the oil gets quite warm.

All of the flat engines burn a small amount of oil, it's nearly impossible to catch all of the splash even with really good oil control rings. It is one of the charming things about the cars."

The 991 GT3

The Porsche 991 GT3 is an over-the-top race car with aggressive styling and an even more aggressive engine and drivetrain. Porsche issued a stop driving notice when a couple of engines burst into flames. The vehicles were practically brand new, which led to lots of speculations of an internal design flaw in the 991 GT3. In 2014, Porsche's Product Manager acknowledged that there was a problem with a connecting rod in the crankcase and replaced 700 engines. In 2015, a new problem with the valve train prompted another recall.

Porsche announced that it replaced the engines on every single 2014 model year GT3 sold--a full 785 vehicles. As recalls go, the correctional measures are fairly extreme--and cost Porsche a fortune, despite the relatively small number of vehicles involved--but could be the best way of curtailing further fire-related embarrassments for the company.

Confessions of a Former Porsche Aficionado

Jack Baruth, an auto writer for thetruthaboutcars.com, has been a Porsche aficionado for many years. Baruth said,

> I am currently the owner of three Porsches, as pathetic as that may be, and I've experienced firsthand the many ways in which Porsche disappoints its fans and buyers. Few companies have been as comprehensively whitewashed by the media and the corporate biographers, but the truth is available to those of us who wish to look a bit harder.

We will start with the big betrayals, of course, and the unassuming fastback you see above represents perhaps the worst of Porsche's many middle fingers to the customer base. It is a 1999 Porsche 911, known to everyone in the world as the "996".

From 1964 to 1998, the 911 evolved on an incremental basis. As with the first and last Volkswagen Beetles, there are very, very few parts which survived the thirty-four-year journey unchanged, but there's an amazing amount of interchangeability.

The 911 was never intended to last thirty-four years. The front-engine, water-cooled 928 was supposed to replace the 911 in the Seventies ... but it didn't, so the 911's lifetime was extended another decade. The costs and inefficiencies of building a car with a Sixties architecture tortured Porsche. A complete re-engineering was necessary, and Porsche worked with Toyota to squeeze every last dollar out of the new 911's design.

> The list of cost-cuts in the Porsche 996 can be recited by nearly every Porschephile. Frameless doors, complete commonality with the Boxster from the door latches forward, horrifying interior trim quality, drop-in assemblies provided by the lowest bidder, and the engine....

Porsche had been fighting problems of the water-cooled engine, which appeared first in the 1997 Boxster, from the very first car that rolled off the line. Baruth said these cars had "Porous engine blocks, intermediate shaft failures... the water-cooled boxers were junk. This is enough for a Deadly Sin — knowingly equipping every naturally-aspirated Boxster and 911 they sold from 1997 to as late as 2008 with failure-prone engines — but, as always, Porsche raised the bar in the customer-screwing department."

During those years, Porsche worked with its dealers to deny warranty claims, place blame on customers, withhold knowledge of fixes, and generally ruin every bit of goodwill they had built up over years.

The Unbelievably High Cost of Routine Maintenance

According to carserviceprices.com, the average cost for a Porsche oil change ranges from $164 to $250. Porsche dealers charge $300 or more for an oil change. An oil change on the uberdangerous Carrera GT costs $3,000. The cost is so high because service providers have to use special ramps to lift the car, as well as special fasteners to ensure that it doesn't fall over during the service. An oil change also requires two specialty oil filters.

Repairpal.com estimates that he average cost for a Porsche 911 brake pad replacement is between $345 and $620. If you need rotors, repairpal estimates brake rotor replacement costs between $791 and $1962. Labor costs are estimated between $88 and $111, while parts are priced between $257 and $509. YourMechanic.com computed estimates that brake-pad replacement costs are between $178 and $351 on a Porsche Cayenne.

The replacement cost for the "Litronic" headlamp assemblies is enough to make an NBA player weep— more than $1,000 for each one.

Even tires for the 911 are expensive, more than $1,000 for a set. Although auto writer Jack Baruth admitted he drove his Porsche hard, he said that his 911 tires lasted only 7,000 miles.

Coolant Leakage

The National Highway Traffic Safety Administration forced Porsche to recall cars for several reasons. The primary culprit was Coolant leaking from a flange on top of the engine caused rear tires to get wet and lose grip while driving on the street. Porsche dealer fixed the problem under warranty. Apparently, this is a common issue with 2002-2012 Porsche 911 Turbo, GT2, and GT3 models

Porsche Lite

The Porsche 996 is the internal designation for the Porsche 911 model manufactured from 1998 to 2004 that came with a new, water-cooled engine. Long-time Porsche fans found the 996 driving experience to be as questionable as the build quality. This was a quiet, flimsy-feeling car that outhandled, out-accelerated, and out-braked the outgoing 993, while never feeling anything like as substantial as its air-cooled predecessor. The flimsy feeling came partly because Porsche cut weight out of the car compared to the previous model.

The men from Stuttgart knew they had a loser on their hands, so the 996 was freshened in 2002 with a more powerful engine, interior fixes, and a facelift. The market value of the used 996 plummeted faster than the 993.

The Widowmaker

Jack Baruth said, "Another rear engine car, the first Porsche 911 Turbo, received its nickname "The Widowmaker" for good reason." With a rearward weight bias, spongy brakes, and an on-off power delivery, the early 911 Turbos were challenging cars to drive. Though man-ageable in experienced hands, older 911s were squirrely under the brakes or off throttle. When coupled with significant turbo lag, lots of torque and only two driven wheels, the car proved too much for most drivers. Though a respected status symbol, the early 911 Turbo was always feared since it claimed the lives of many drivers and a few celebrities, including NHL goalie Pelle Lindbergh. After a series of wrongful death lawsuits in the late 1970s, Porsche had to offer driver training programs for those who purchased a 911 Turbo. Achtung!

I wondered how many celebrities of some form or fashion have lost their lives while driving or riding in a Porsche street car. I know they've had the nickname of "Widow-maker" for some models, I wondered how true that was.

By now, many of you have probably learned of the passing of actor and *Fast and the Furious* staple, Paul Walker. It was perhaps tragically ironic that Walker died in a fiery, single-vehicle car crash, as a passenger in a 2005 Porsche Carrera GT. He was attending an event for his own charity, Reach Out World Wide, which helps raise funds to send emergency responders to disaster-stricken areas. Walker's career was notable for a number of roles, including starting alongside James Van Der Beek in the 1999 film, *Varsity Blues*. But arguably his most notable role is as Brian O'Connor, the street-racing undercover cop that goes native in the 2001 film, *The Fast and the Furious*. In the motoring world, Walker's name was synonymous with the tuner community, and Walker backed that up by being a true driving enthusiast. After the filming the first movie, Walker acquired an R34 Nissan Skyline GT-R. Reports vary as to whether it was one of the GT-Rs used in the filming of the first or second film. What is certain is that he cared about cars, and had a robust collection that included multiple Lamborghinis, a vintage Corvette and Mustang, and a Ferrari F40. He was even a driver on Redline Time Attack, a racing series in which he piloted a BMW M3.

At the time of the crash, Walker was a passenger in a 2005 Porsche Carrera GT, the German automaker's previous range-topping hypercar before the new 918 Spyder. Walker's friend, Roger Rodas, who owned Always Evolving Performance Motors, where Walker's charity event was being held, was driving the Porsche. We are sad to report that Rodas also passed in the fiery crash, and officials say speed was a factor in the incident.

It is just the latest in a history of celebrity car crashes, and one of several to involve very specialized Porsches. The first and most notable one was that of James Dean in 1955. Dean was driving a race-prepped Porsche 550 Spyder, at speeds of 85 mph (in context, that would have been like driving at speeds close to 120 mph today). The "Little Bastard" as Dean Called his 550 was a lightweight racecar, with minimal (if any) safety features.

James Dean, inset, and the wreckage of his "Little Bastard."

In 1955, there would have been few safety features available that would have helped a driver survive such an incident, but even the advancements in safety technology half-century were not enough to help *Jackass* star Ryan Dunn.

Sometime after 3:00am, on June 20, 2011, Dunn and a Jackass production assistant, Zachary Hartwell entered Dunn's late-model Porsche 911 GT3. Their late night joyride ended with the high-performance Porsche slam-ming into a tree at speeds between 132 and 140 mph. Toxicology reports would later determine that Dunn's blood alcohol content was more than twice the Pennsylvania state legal limit.

I am not saying that the choice of Porsche vehicle was the cause of, or contributed to, the crash (In Dunn's case, we're certain of that). But in these three incidents, automotive thrill-seekers selected a rare, high-performance Porsche their vehicle of choice. Consider the tires in a situation like this. Though there is a possibility the vehicle was modified, images from the crash reveal that the wheels appear to be stock, so there is a good chance the tires could still be the Michelin tires that are sized only for the GT. Typically, the Michelin Pilot Sport 2 tires that would be on a stock Carrera GT are a soft compound that warms up quickly and offers serious grip, but until they are warm, do not offer full traction. It is not uncommon for even a seasoned driver to loose traction if driving too fast on tires that are not appropriately warmed up.

With time, more details will come out regarding the Walker-Rodas crash. But the common thread among all these crashes was that they took lives that many looked to for laughter, drama, and entertainment. From Dean, to Dunn to Walker, their work, in one way or another, touched many lives. The other common thread among all three– their lives were taken far too soon.

Porsche Carrera GT

A car company worker sent emails in 2006 revealing "as many as 200" Porsche 1280 Carrera GTs had been "totaled" in the two years since its release, *TMZ* reported.

Paul, 40, was a passenger in a 2005 Carrera GT at the time of his 2013 death, which means the vehicle was manufactured during the period in question. Despite all this carnage, the unnamed employee claims these accidents were good for business for one disturbing reason.

The *Fast & the Furious* actor was in a Carrera GT when it swerved out of control and also hit a lamppost and tree, as opposed to a telephone pole. The sports car then burst into flames with the father of one inside. It sounds as if the Porsche employees had this kind of deadly scene in their own minds while driving the vehicles, but didn't publicize that information. "Any ethical company would have withdrawn the car from the market," attorney Jeffrey Milam says in the middle of a wrongful death lawsuit against Porsche. "Or, at the very least, warned the public about its dangers."

Chapter Six

Audi

"In fact, the only firm whose cars had a worse engine failure rate than Audi was MG Rover."

—Auto Express (U.K.)

WarrantyWise found that Audis were very unreliable. In their list of most reliable manufacturers, Audi came in 28th out of 36 companies. This dependability rating was based on the number of reported faults or breakdowns. This is from data WarrantyWise collected, and they are a company that provides used car warranties. Their pool of data might not be as large as that of *Consumer Reports* and J.D Power, but it is based on actual repairs, not just consumer surveys.

There isn't one particular reason why Audi's are unreliable. However, there is a trend when it comes to luxury cars and that is that the electronics let them down. Audis come with lots of modern technology, and it can be that modern technology that breaks down. If the technology is quite new or just complex, it can come with it's own set of problems. This is what many put down as the reason for Audi's unreliability problems.

If you are looking at buying an Audi for the long term, or perhaps you are looking at buying a used Audi, then you will want to know what sort of problems you may encounter further down the line. Some common Audi problems you may find tens of thousands of miles in could include:

Oil Leaks

- Audi engines tend to leak from valve covers or tensioner gasket seals.
- Obviously, an oil leak can be a fire hazard. So if this is happening to your Audi, then you should get it fixed as soon as possible.

Exhaust Leaks

- This is often a problem because most Audi models have a flexible joint in the exhaust. This joint is prone to wear and can leak.

Those are two of the most common problems that you tend to find with an Audi. As we said, these only really become problems when your model is several thousand miles in. But if you are looking at a used Audi model, then these are some things you might want to be looking out for.

It's not only Audi that have had to fend off reports of unreliability, their German counterparts have also suffered from claims of unreliability. But, which out of Audi, BMW and Mercedes is more reliable?

In the *Consumer Reports* scorecard in which-- Audi came top, BMW came in the top five, but Mercedes came 14th. In the WarrantyWise survey, BMW came in 29th. Not that Audi and Mercedes did much better, they came 28th and 27th respectively.

If we look at J.D Power, then Audi is higher than BMW and Mercedes, and this is the same with the *Which? Reports*.

Which Audis are the Least Reliable?

Historically, the least dependable Audi models have been the following:

- Audi Q5

- Audi Q7

- Audi A3

These cars all scored less than 3 out of 5 according to J.D Power. Audi certainly isn't the most reliable brand on the market, with their technology letting them down. Their engines are also not as reliable as many people think, not even reaching the top ten in the WarrantyWise survey. It is also difficult to tell how reliable their latest models will be as the results are not yet in for long-term dependability.

Audis aren't horrifically unreliable nor are they the most reliable brand out there. One thing is certain, however, and that's that Audi have consistently scored high performance, so whether you can sacrifice top reliability for a high-performance luxury car, is up to your personal choice.

Repair Costs

RepairPal.com states, "The Audi Reliability Rating is 3.0 out of 5.0, which ranks it 29th out of 32 for all car brands. This rating is based on an average across 345 unique models. The average annual repair cost for a Audi is $1,011, which means it has average ownership costs. The other factors that contribute to Audi reliability include an average of 1.0 visits to a repair shop per year and a 10% probability of a repair being severe. The average annual repair cost for all Audi models is $1,011 per year, compared to $631 across all models. This includes both scheduled maintenance and unscheduled repair." This is less than BMW and Mercedes, but higher that most cars.

In 2017 RepairPal created its Reliability Rating based on actual vehicle repairs. For 2018, the updated RepairPal Reliability Rating has analyzed millions of repair orders from over 2,000 auto shops across the country, measuring dependability by evaluating the cost, frequency and severity of repairs.

While other reliability scores are based on subjective results from consumer surveys, RepairPal's Reliability Rating uses real-world data to help consumers seek out the best car for them. It is similar to ratings from

WarrantyWise because they both use actual repair data, not consumer surveys.

The Reliability Rating by RepairPal is a measurement of vehicle dependability based on the cost, frequency, and severity of unscheduled repairs and maintenance. Repair Pal combines an extensive proprietary database including millions of vehicle repair invoices with additional automotive statistics and predictive data science to develop the most genuine reliability metric in the industry. Cars included in the Reliability Rating cover 2010-2017 model year vehicles with controls in place to ensure statistical confidence.

Your Mechanic rated the Audi the fifth most expensive car to maintain per ten years at an average of $12,400 in repair costs. The BMW came in first at $17,800, the Mercedes second at $12,900. VW was 22nd at $7,800. Toyota, at 30th place, was the cheapest to maintain at $5,500 over a ten-year period.

Consumer Reports echoed the results of *Your Mechanic* finding BMW the most expensive car to maintain, Mer-cedes the second most expensive and Audi the third most expensive over a ten-year period. Volkswagen was about average.

Forbes magazine studied car repair costs and reported, "At the top of our list of the most expensive luxury vehicles to repair are the Audi A8 and Mercedes-Benz G Class, both with five-year estimated repair costs of $1,640. Rounding out the luxury vehicles in the top five are the Jaguar XK, at $1,629; Land Rover Range Rover, at $1,600; and Mercedes-Benz CL at $1,540." *Forbes* based their results on repair estimates calculated over a five-year period by Vincentric, an auto-industry data-analysis company. Vincentric looked at the cost of zero-deductible, bumper-to-bumper extended-warranty claims to calculate the average cost owners can expect to pay for repairs. Their estimates do not include maintenance, which Vincentric measures separately.

Audis, for example, according to an Audi technician in Los Angeles, have electronic sensors on their brakes, so replacing their brake pads are more complicated and take more time to install. The hourly labor cost will vary, but brake work on an **Audi** may cost $250 without labor, compared with $150 on a non-luxury vehicle

Safety

In late 2018 it was announced that Audi is recalling about 1.2 million cars and SUVs worldwide because the electric coolant pumps can overheat and possibly cause a fire. The models affected are the Audi A4, A5, A6 and Q5 with the 2.0l TFSI engine, produced between 2012 and 2017.

The "Audis burning" story is to a large extent being driven on social media by Capetonian Themba Mabasa, who has gone head-on with Audi South Africa since his three-year-old Audi TT burnt out completely during a long road trip from Cape Town to Limpopo on the Easter weekend in 2018.

Elizabeth Avery had just heard about a Global News story about a man whose 2011 Audi Q5 burst into flames on a Toronto highway. The report showed a ball of flame consuming Chris Sahadeo's SUV, which had just left his auto dealer after scheduled repairs.

"I feel like I almost died," Sahadeo told Global News in October 2015, moments after watching in disbelief as his pricey German-made car burned beyond recognition.

Elizabeth Avery had just heard about a Global News story about a man whose 2011 Audi Q5 burst into flames on a Toronto highway.

The report showed a ball of flame consuming Chris Sahadeo's SUV, which had just left his auto dealer after scheduled repairs.

"I could see smoke billowing out the front of the vehicle," said Avery. "There were flames shooting out everywhere." Luckily, Avery and a family member were able to extinguish the flames, confined to the engine compartment. A subsequent investigation by her insurance company concluded that the cause of the fire was related to the Audi's coolant pump. At the time, Avery reported the problem to Audi Canada, hoping the company would take the matter seriously. She says she was ignored.

"I feel like I almost died," Sahadeo told Global News in October 2015, moments after watching in disbelief as his pricey German-made car burned beyond recognition. A subsequent investigation by her insur-ance company concluded that the cause of the fire was related to the Audi's coolant pump.

About 135,000 Porsche and Volkswagen sport utilities were recalled over the danger of a fuel leak, according to documents from the automakers posted on the website of the National Highway Traffic Safety Administration. In its report Porsche said the action covers about 50,000 vehicles. They are the-- Porsche 2004-06 Cayenne, 2003-06 Cayenne S and 2003-06 Cayenne Turbo. Volkswagen told federal regulators about 74,000 2004-07 Touareg models are covered.

The automakers' reports did not mention that have been many fires. The recalls come about a year after

Themba Mabasa three-year-old Audi went up in flames on the side of a Gauteng freeway on Easter Friday.

Audi re-called about 143,000 corporate siblings, the 2009-12 Q5 and 2007-12 Q7 for the same problem. That problem is that "fine hairline cracks can appear, after an extended period of use, on the filter flange of the fuel pump," the automaker said. That would allow "a very small quantity" of fuel to leak.

At the time, Avery reported the problem to Audi Canada, hoping the company would take the matter seriously. She says she was ignored. Veteran automobile technician Kirk Robinson, who owns a repair facility in Mississauga, Ontario, says safety is a key concern for car and truck owners.

"They want to know their vehicle is safe–they want to have confidence in their service provider and the manufacturer of their vehicle," said Robinson, who has for years also hosted an automobile help program on a local cable television channel.

Robinson says some manufacturers are more transparent that others when dealing with consumer complaints about safety, and he points to an example involving his shop. "I've had a car come in here from a manufacturer–it had an explosion on the engine. I had to prove it was a manufacturer's defect. And the manufacturer paid it out, very quietly," he said.

Audi Canada finally acknowledged Avery's concerns about the overall safety of her repaired vehicle. The company agreed to replace it after a Global News story and other pressure, she said. Avery says the company asked her not to tell anyone, but did not bind her by a non-disclosure agreement.

Eighteen months after her vehicle burned and she attempted to get the company to pay attention, she's concerned Audi did too little, too late. She says consumers have to keep pressure on companies that don't appear to take safety seriously enough. Avery said, "Consumers have to make sure the problem is dealt with. Not only dealt with but that other people know it."

Volkswagen AG is adding almost 300,000 Porsche and Audi vehicles to a previous recall for a fuel-pump defect that could result in fire, according to the U.S. National Highway Traffic Safety Administration. About 135,000 Porsche and Volkswagen sport utilities were recalled over the danger of a fuel leak, according to documents from the automakers posted on the website of the National Highway Traffic Safety Administration.

In its report Porsche said the action covers about 50,000 vehicles. They are the Porsche 2004-06 Cayenne, 2003-06 Cayenne S and 2003-06 Cayenne Turbo. Volkswagen told federal regulators about 74,000 2004-07 Touareg models are covered.

The automaker's reports did not mention whether there were any fires. The recalls came about a year after Audi recalled about 143,000 corporate siblings, the 2009-12 Q5 and 2007-12 Q7 for the same problem.

That problem is that "fine hairline cracks can appear, after an extended period of use, on the filter flange of the fuel pump," the automaker said. That would allow "a very small quantity" of fuel to leak.

The fuel-pump flange on certain Porsche Macan models and Audi Q5 and Q7 sport-utility vehicles may crack, which may lead to a fuel leak and possibly result in a fire, the auto-safety regulator said in recall advisories posted Saturday to its website. The components were manufactured by Continental AG.

The Audi Q5s were built from July 2012 to March 2017, and the Q7s between May 2012 and July 2015. Dealers will apply a protective film to the fuel pump component, or replace it if cracks are found. The recall is set to begin July 2.

About 240,500 Audis and 51,500 Porsches are affected by the recalls. Porsche Cars North America is recalling certain Macan S and Macan Turbo vehicles from model years 2015 to 2017, as well as 2017 Macan, Macan Turbo with Performance Package and Macan GTS vehicles. The same remedies will apply to the Porsches.

A second recall of Audi vehicles and SUVs was announced in 2018 amid reports of fires due to overheating in the vehicles. The affected vehicles include 342,867 cars in the United States and 50,000 cars in Canada. The recall is aimed at vehicles with 2.0-liter Turbo FSI engines including the 2013-2017 A5 and Q5, the 2013-2016 A4 sedan and Allroad, and 2012-2015 A6 vehicles with four-cylinder Turbo FSI engines.

Volkswagen became aware of the risk of fires from over-heating back in 2015. Audi had been notified about several cases where engine parts spontaneously began to fume. In 2017, Audi issued a recall of more than one million vehicles due to defective electric coolant pumps. In certain vehicles, the pump was blocked by debris from the cooling system which led to spontaneous fires. Moisture issues in the coolant pump that could cause a short circuit were also blamed for the recall. Audi announced a software update to repair the problem. But even after new software was installed, some cars continued to experience spontaneous explosions. Audi then announced a second recall of approximately 1.2 million vehicles to repair the issue again.

This time Audi announced that it will take a more aggressive approach to addressing this defect by replacing the pump with a new, updated version. In addition, the car manufacturer plans to introduce a reconfigured pump, but that part will not be available until November of this year. Audi informed the National High-way Traffic Safety Administration (NHTSA) that it in-tends to replace the defective pumps immediately and then install the redesigned pumps in the fall once they are available. The pumps will be replaced free of charge to car owners. With this final repair, Audi owners will have brought their cars to the dealer three times to rectify this fire hazards.

While Audi informed the NHTSA of fires in several of the affected vehicles, it did not report any injuries or deaths resulting from this defect. As always, car owners should check whether their vehicles are affected by the recall by looking up their car's VIN number and proceeding with repair instructions if their car is involved in the recall.

Audi A4

The Audi A4 is one of the most popular and least expenisve Audis. J.D. Power Initial Quality ranks the A4 only 2 out of 5. During the crash test of the A4, the footrest and instrument panel moved toward the driver, making injuries to the left hip likely in the event of an accident. The dummy's head did hit the front airbag but slid off to the left side, while the side torso airbag did not deploy. Furthermore, the driver door opened during the crash, placing the driver at risk of being ejected from the vehicle.

Dieselgate

The EPA discovered Dieselgate emissions-cheating software in 2015, and then a German team found more evidence in 2016, and then in 2017 the German Transport Ministry is recalling 24,000 Audi A7 and A8s for the same reason.

The A8 is Audi's top-of-the-line car, and despite VW's insistence that its cheating software doesn't violate EU law, the German ministry has given the company a deadline to form "a comprehensive plan to refit the cars."

When Audi's headquarters were raided by prosecutors in 2017 in connection with the emissions fraud, Chief Executive Rupert Stadler said investigations into the scandal were far from over, promising to keep at it until the work was done.

A source close to Audi said problems in the interaction between transmission and engine control units are to blame for the emissions overshoot. A proposal for a fix has already been submitted to the KBA, the source said, declining to elaborate.

Chapter Seven

Volkswagen

"It is for the broad masses that this car has been built. Its purpose is to answer their transportation needs, and it is intended to give them joy." –

Adolf Hitler

In 1937, the government of Germany—then under the control of Adolf Hitler of the National Socialist (Nazi) Party—formed a new state-owned automobile company, then known as Gesellschaft zur Vorbereitung des Deutschen Volkswagens mbH. Later that year, it was renamed simply Volkswagenwerk, or "The People's Car Company."

Originally operated by the German Labor Front, a Nazi organization, Volkswagen was headquartered in Wolfsburg, Germany. In addition to his ambitious campaign to build a network of autobahns and limited access highways across Germany, Hitler's pet project was the development and mass production of an affordable vehicle that could sell for less than 1,000 Reich marks (about $140 at the time). To provide the design for his "people's car," Hitler called in automotive engineer Ferdinand Porsche. In 1938, at a Nazi rally, the Fuhrer declared: "It is for the broad masses that this car has been built. Its purpose is to answer their transportation needs, and it is intended to give them joy."

However, soon after the KdF (Kraft-durch-Freude)-Wagen ("Strength-Through-Joy" car) was displayed for the first time at the Berlin Motor Show in 1939, World War II began, and Volkswagen halted production. After the war ended, with the factory in ruins, the Allies would make Volkswagen the focus of their attempts to resuscitate the German auto industry.

After the war, Volkswagen sales in the United States were initially slower than in other parts of the world, due to the car's historic Nazi connections as well as its small size unsuited to American roads. In 1959, the advertising agency Doyle Dane Bernbach launched a landmark campaign, dubbing the car the "Beetle" and spinning its diminutive size as a distinct advantage to consumers. Over the next several years, VW became the top-selling auto im-port in the United States.

Twelve years later in 1971, the Beetle surpassed the longstanding worldwide production record of 15 million vehicles, set by Ford Motor Company's legendary Model T between 1908 and 1927.

With the Beetle's design relatively unchanged since 1935, sales grew sluggish in the early 1970s. VW bounced back with the introduction of sportier models such as the Rabbit and later, the Golf. In 1998, the company began selling the highly touted "New Beetle" while still continuing production of its predecessor. After nearly 70 years and more than 21 million units produced, the last original Beetle rolled off the line in Puebla, Mexico, on July 30, 2003.

Sales in the United States were 293,595 in 1980, but by 1984 they were down to 177,709.

Volkswagen Today

Volkswagen is the founding and namesake member of the Volkswagen Group, a large international corporation in charge of multiple car and truck brands, including Audi, SEAT, Porsche, Lamborghini, Bentley, Bugatti, Scania, MAN, and Škoda. Volkswagen Group's global headquarters are located in Volkswagen's historic home of Wolfsburg, Germany.

Volkswagen Group, as a unit, is Europe's largest automaker. For a long time, Volkswagen has had a European market share over 20 percent. In 2010, Volkswagen posted record global sales of 6.29 million vehicles, with its global market share at 11.4%. Since 2012, Volkswagen is the second largest manufacturer worldwide to number one Toyota.

In 2008, Porsche revealed its plan to assume control of VW. As of that year, it owned 42.6% of Volkswagen's shares and stock options on another 31.5%. By January 2009, Porsche had a 50.76% holding in Volkswagen AG, although the "Volkswagen Law" prevented it from taking control of the company.

In May 2009, the two companies decided to join together, in a merger. Volkswagen announced that its percentage in Porsche would be 49.9% for a cost of €3.9 billion (the 42.0% deal would have cost €3.3 billion).

J.D. Power survey: Everybody kind of expects Volkswagen to be at the bottom of the reliability charts, so it's no surprise to see them here ranked 19th of the 31 brands in the list. Volkswagen actually improved its score from 164 to 157, and jumped up one spot on the brand rankings, but it seems about par for the course for VW to land slightly below average. It certainly didn't help that one of their most popular lines, the Golf and GTI, launched an entirely new generation (Mk 7) and advanced MQB platform as 2015 models in North America, not to mention a new diesel powertrain in their best-selling Jetta.

Are Volkswagens Reliable?

A study by Warranty Direct found that consumers believe German cars are much more reliable than they actually are, including Volkswagen's. A survey by WarrantyDirect found that Volkswagens were ninth in terms of unreliability, with 1 in 52 engines resulting in failure. In-terestingly, this is better than their German coun-terparts, Audi and BMW, with a failure rate of 1 in 27 and 1 in 45 respectively. J.D Power ranks Volkswagen even lower than the Warraty Direct survey, ranking them 2 out of 5 for overall dependability. This puts them in "The Rest" category, which is not the category you want to be in.

The *Consumer Reports* survey of 2016 says very similar. It ranks Volkswagen as 22nd out of 29th for reliability with a reliability score of just 30 out of 100. This is down nine places from last year. The average reliability score for this survey is between 41 and 60, so Volkswagen are pretty well below average in this case.

Consumer Reports have noted that Volkswagen has had problems with the four and five-cylinder engines found in the Jetta, Passat, and some other models.

Why are Volkswagen's Unreliable?

Consumer Reports reported faults with the engines in some VW models including the Passat and Jetta, so much of their unreliability stem from their engine designs. Based on consumer surveys and the consumer feedback, much of Volkswagen's unreliability sits with its engines, rather than its technology like many of its

German counterparts. Warranty Direct gathers their information from the 50,000 extended warranties they have provided to customers.

In the Warranty Direct survey, Toyota came in second for reliability, with only 1 in 171 engines resulting in failure. Ford didn't do as well, but still came in the top ten in eighth place. Warranty Direct found that 1 in 80 cars resulted in engine failure. This is considerably better than Volkswagen who came ninth for most unreliable with a 1 in 52 failure rate.

The 2017 *Consumer Reports* survey also put Toyota in second place for reliability, giving it a reliability rating of 78 out of 100. Again, this is better than both Ford and Volkswagen. Ford didn't fare too badly, just scraping into the 'reliable' category at 18th and a reliability rating of 44. As we mentioned above, Volkswagen didn't do too well at all, coming in 22nd with a reliability rating of 30.

Compared to Ford and Toyota, Volkswagen are pretty unreliable. However, Toyotas are extremely reliable, and are renowned for their reliability. So Ford and Volks-wagen were never really going to come off looking good when compared to the brand. That said,

Volkswagen still didn't do as well as Ford and has come across looking distinctly below average.

Which Volkswagen Cars are the Least Reliable?

The following models are the ones that are the least reli-able Volkswagen models;

- 2014 Volkswagen CC
- 2010 Volkswagen Touareg
- 2013 Volkswagen CC

These all scored 2 out of 5 on J.D Power for predicted re-liability. So, are Volkswagens really unreliable? It de-pends what model you go for. As you can see, the Tiguan has done well on J.D Power, and many drivers say that the Golf is a very reliable car. But, the Volkswagen CC and the Passat have not fared as well, and their reliability is very much below average. As a whole, Volkswagen hasn't scored highly on dependability.

Safety

The Insurance Institute for Highway Safety issued a crit-ical report, "The [Volkswagen] CC is the first vehicle the institute has ever evaluated to completely lose its door." IIHS explained that any vehicle that loses its door automatically fails a test as the driver could be ejected from the vehicle.

Volkswagen also issued extensive recall of it Tiguan model concerning fire risk. VW's latest of 700,000 vehicles worldwide it does qualify as a fairly extensive one. According to German publication KFZ-Betrieb, the vehicles affected are 2018 Tiguan and Touran models equipped with a panoramic roof and ambient lighting. The recall states that the LED strip installed is not insulated properly and humidity can cause a short circuit in the system, or in rare instances cause the unit to catch on fire.

In 2013, a Touareg owner from California wrote federal officials about a "puddle" of gas beneath his vehicle, noting "this is a serious problem and has to be addressed before someone dies. It is a hazard to my family and the public as a whole." It appears that many Volkswagen SUVs have safety and fire issues. Volkswagen told the U.S. National Highway Traffic

Safety Administration that about 74,000 2004-07 Touareg models are being recalled for fuel leaks.

About 135,000 Porsche and Volkswagen sport utilities are being recalled over the danger of a fuel leak, according to documents from the automakers posted on the website of the National Highway Traffic Safety Administration.

Chapter Eight

Other German Products

Germany still makes many high-quality products. They are known for their knives, including Henckels and Wustof. But knives of comparable quality are made by American, French and English knife makers, such as Lamson (made in Shelburne Falls, Massachusetts since 1837), Sabatier (made in Thiers, France since 1834) and Aron-dight (England). Consumer reviews in Amazon are comparable for all of these knife makers.

Similarly, Bosch and Miele, German appliance manufacturers make high-quality products. However comparable appliances are made in other countries. I chuckled when I read that Wolf products were German. They are actually made in the USA, but apparently some stores think that they are German because of their high quality and possibly German name. American-made Dacor also competes well with the German brands.

When we get into larger products, the Germans have had some spectacular failures. These failures include German warships, concert halls and subways.

Germany's naval brass in 2005 dreamed up a warship that could ferry marines into combat anywhere in the world, go up against enemy ships and stay away from home ports for two years with a crew half the size of its predecessor's. First delivered for sea trials in 2016 after a series of delays, the 7,000-ton Baden-Württemberg frigate was determined last month to have an unexpected design flaw: It doesn't really work.

Defense experts cite the warship's buggy software and ill-considered arsenal—as well as what was until recently its noticeable list to starboard—as symptoms of deeper, more intractable problems: Shrinking military expertise and growing confusion among German leaders about what the country's armed forces are for.

A litany of bungled infrastructure projects has tarred Germany's reputation for engineering prowess. There is still no opening date for Berlin's new €6 billion ($7.2 billion) airport, which is already 10 years behind schedule, and the redesign of Stuttgart's railway station remains stalled more than a decade after work on the project started. Observers have blamed these mishaps on poor planning and project management, which also figured in major setbacks for several big military pro-jects.

Germany's Main Warship Puts On Weight But Loses Effectiveness

During World War II the German Navy was dominant, sinking American and British warships almost at will. The current German Navy is not so fierce.

Germany's next-generation F-125 frigate is supposed to replace the F-122, but naval experts report that it lacks the firepower to defend Baltic Sea lanes against the Russian navy or to counter well-armed terrorists.

But experts say military efforts have also been hampered by the lack of a strategic vision for Germany's armed forces, resulting in vague, hard-to-execute briefs. Before the frigate project foundered, a contract to build a new helicopter hit snags, costs for a new rifle overran and an ambitious drone project simply failed to get off the ground.

German military procurement is "one hell of a complete disaster," said Christian Mölling, a defense-industry ex-pert at the German Council on Foreign Relations in Berlin. "It will take years to sort this problem out."

The naval fiasco, on a project with a €3 billion price tag, is particularly startling since Europe's largest exporter relies on open and secure shipping lanes to transport its goods.

The F-125 frigate program was supposed to deliver Germany's four largest military ships of the postwar era, fitted with cutting-edge software allowing high opera-bility with a skeleton crew. But after the ship failed sea trials last month, naval officials refused to commission it. The German Navy said the Baden-Württemberg's central computer system—the design centerpiece allowing it to sail with a smaller crew—didn't pass necessary tests. The Kieler Nachrichten, a daily in the German Baltic fleet's home port of Kiel, has reported problems with its radar, electronics and the flameproof coating on its fuel tanks. The vessel was also found to list to the starboard, a flaw a project spokesman says has been corrected. The Baden-Württemberg is now set to return to port next week for an "extended period," the navy said.

A spokesman for Thyssenkrupp, the lead company on the project, said it still planned to deliver the ship this year. "The frigate-class 125 is a newly designed, technically sophisticated ship with highly complex new developments—including new technologies," the spokesman said. "Delays can never be completely ruled out." A spokesman for the military procurement office said it was levying financial penalties from Thyssenkrupp for late delivery, but he declined to provide further details.

Even if the ship can be fixed, however, some naval experts worry it would struggle to defend itself against terrorist groups supplied with anti-ship missiles. And in the face of a Russian naval buildup in the Baltic Sea, it lacks its predecessor's sonar and torpedo tubes, making it a sitting duck for submarines.

Those failings, they say, result from Germany's military brass never settling on a defined brief for the vessel. When planning began in 2003, naval staff wanted an all-rounder that could tangle with Russian destroyers in the Baltic and serve as a base for humanitarian missions in tropical waters. Then, in 2005, they decided the ship didn't need all of its predecessor's heavy weaponry and should focus more on attacking enemies on land, including by ferrying marines into combat.

Given Russia's aggressive stance in the Baltic Sea, naval experts say that now appears to have been a miscalculation. The ship's great weight—already almost twice that of the frigate model it is replacing—makes adding further weapons very difficult. "These problems stem from Germany not having a strategic vision for its military," said Ronja Kempin, defense-industry expert at the German Institute for International and Security Affairs in Berlin.

Defense experts say the frigate fiasco also shows the navy, German military engineers and the government's de-fense-procurement body, after years without big projects to manage, has lost the expertise to bring these to fruition. "Too complicated, too ambitious, too badly managed." Marcel Dickow, a weapons-procurement ex-pert at the German Institute for International and Security Affairs in Berlin, said of the frigate. "They threw money at the project without thinking it through."

The spokesman for Germany's military procurement office said while the ship project posed an "enormous challenge" for the contractors, its design specifications were "unambiguous and precise." He added that the contractors have to solve outstanding problems with the vessel. "The [German military] will not take over the ship until all acceptance trials have been successfully completed," he said.

German military spending is now rising rapidly to meet the North Atlantic Treaty Organization's agreed commitment of 2% of gross domestic product. The defense budget is set to climb to €38.5 billion in 2018 from €37 billion in 2017 and €35.1 billion in 2016.

'There's a whole generation of German engineers who haven't worked on a major defense project. It's not that they lost this skill; they never learned it." Said Christian Mölling, German Council on Foreign Relations.

But this growth follows years of fiscal attrition that have degraded the government's capacity to manage ambitious military projects. And while German firms like Heckler & Koch AG and Rheinmetall are market leaders in rifles, tanks and howitzers, competence in larger, more complex systems has eroded during the lean years.

"There's a whole generation of German engineers who haven't worked on a major defense project," said Mr.

Mölling, the defense expert. "It's not that they lost this skill; they never learned it."

Engineering graduates shun weapons manufacturers in favor of "sexier" employers like conglomerate Siemens AG or auto company BMW AG, which offer better pay and career prospects, according to Mr. Mölling.

Likewise, defense companies have failed to attract the graduates needed to develop sophisticated new systems that are increasingly centered on software, said Sandro Gaycken, a director at the European School of Man-agement and Technology in Berlin.

Berlin could have bought warships from U.S., U.K. or French shipyards, but the government chose German bidders to buoy employment at German shipyards, according to Ms. Kempin, the defense expert.

Kiel-based naval engineer Lothar Dannenberg, who was not involved directly in the frigate project, blamed its failures largely on what he said was the incompetence of the procurement office. "We were left shaking our heads," he said.

German Engineering on Land

German engineering on land, roads and buildings had been excellent for many decades. German railroads were notoriously punctual. General Dwight David Eisenhower was so impressed with the German autobahns during World War II that he successfully pushed for the U.S. interstate highway system when he became president of the United States in the 1950s. However, things have changed. German construction projects are now routinely late, often by many years, and way over budget.

If you visit downtown Leipzig you may travel through the City Tunnel. The tunnel is part of the city's new 1.5 kilometer (0.93 miles) project designed to move commuter trains more quickly through the city's Central Station, which is a terminus station. The project was sup-posed to be completed in 2009 at a cost of €572 million. Instead, it cost €960 million and opened in December, 2013, four years late.

In the capital of the state of Baden-Württemberg, the Stuttgart 21 project was supposed to transform the city's terminus into a modern underground station. The project's planner, German national railway Deutsche Bahn, originally estimated total costs to be €2.5

billion. In 2008, the state's then-governor said costs had risen to €3.1 billion, but the project had been "planned solidly." Just a few months later, federal auditors estimated the project would cost "clearly more than €5.3 billion." In 2009, the city, state and federal governments agreed to a ceiling of €4.5 billion. By December 2012, however, it became clear that costs could soar to €6.8 billion, assuming the station goes into operation, as planned, by 2021. Deutsche Bahn executives claim it will cost a maximum of €5.6 billion and that the company will cover the bill.

However, the company said there are also €1.2 billion in "external risks" caused by mass protests against the project and changes made to accommodate critics. It is still unclear who will pay that bill. So far, city and state officials are refusing to cover those costs.

Bah Hamburg

New York has the Statue of Liberty, Paris has the Eiffel Tower, and Berlin has the Brandenburg Gate. In Hamburg, the city would like its new symphony hall, the Elbphilharmonie designed by Swiss architects Herzog and de Meuron, to be its most iconic landmark. The structure, proudly located at the western end of the wealthy new HafenCity district along the Elbe River, also includes 45 luxury apartments, a parking lot and a five-star hotel. The city hired a consortium under the leadership of massive German construction company Hochtief to do the job in 2007. A price of €241 million had been agreed to at the time, with the city of Hamburg liable for €142 million. The concert hall was scheduled to open in 2010, but the building is nowhere near complete today. The construction site sat still for nearly a year as the city, Hochtief and the architects fought over costs, safety concerns and the delays. At the end of 2012, Hochtief and the city agreed to a new price tag: €575 million. It is still unclear how much of that bill taxpayers will end up paying. Hamburg's symphony finally opened Elbphil-harmonie in January, 2017, seven years late and more than double its original cost.

Cologne's North-South Subway Line

Problems related to the construction of a new subway line in Cologne are equally as notorious as those pertaining to Berlin's airport. Construction of the city's new line began in 2004, but the project has been afflicted with major and deadly problems. Part of the tunnel collapsed in 2009, taking the city's archive building and many of its historical documents and artifacts with it. Two people died in the incident and it caused about €1 billion in damages. So far, no party has been blamed for the accident.

In 2000, the estimated cost for the project was €600 million, but today it has soared to €1.04 billion. Part of the line has already opened, but no date has been given for when the entire route will be operational, and it could be 2019 or even 2022 before it is. City planners have potentially bigger worries this week. The part of the line that opened in December runs right next to Cologne's landmark cathedral, a UNESCO World Heritage site. Church officials claim trains running along the line are causing the massive structure to vibrate. "It cannot be ruled out that the (vibrations) could cause long-term damage to the structure," church Provost Norbert Feldhoff warned.

Munich's Second Commuter Rail Tunnel

For years, officials in Munich have been debating the best way to alleviate the bottleneck occurring in the tunnel on the city's suburban railway line between the central and Ostbahnhof stations. In November, 2013, the city, the state of Bavaria and the federal government reached an agreement to build a second tunnel that would go into operation by 2020. At the time, the costs were estimated to be €2.047 billion.

This time, officials added a €500 million buffer to address any cost overruns. But an internal paper from September, 2012 suggested project costs had already risen to €2.433 billion, a sum that would consume a good chunk of the additional funding. Documents relating to the permit-issuing process assume the tunnel will first be completed in 2021 or 2022. The state government has been outraged by the increase, but planners say they are just providing "an extremely conservative estimate" in the event of delays in construction or receiving permits, and possible legal issues.

The Egg is Dented

Knick-Ei ("dented egg") was the nickname of a sports hall located at the corner of Feldstraße and Bahnhofstraße in the city of Halstenbek, in-- Pinneberg county in the state of Schleswig-Holstein in northern Germany. The nickname refers to the hall's dome-shaped roof which collapsed twice during construction. The sports hall was never operational and was eventually demolished in 2007. The building's official name was "Sporthalle Feldstraße."

In June 1998, two months before the scheduled opening at the beginning of the new school year, the dome, which had been completed in the meantime, collapsed again. This time, the city of Halstenbek's administration filed lawsuits against all companies involved in the construction in order to determine who was responsible and liable for the damage caused by the collapse.

The Battle of Berlin

In Berlin, the city is planning to rebuild its historic Stadtschloss, the palace that was badly damaged during World War II and later torn down in 1950 by East German authorities. The project has long been the subject of controversy because of its cost and the suggestion that Berlin is looking to the past, rather than its future. The structure, to be named the Humboldt Forum, is to house works from the city's collection of art and historical artifacts. Agreed to in 2007, the palace was scheduled to rise again by 2012. Instead, it has been plagued with delays and soaring costs. Costs were initially estimated at €552 million in 2007, but the German federal parliament has already approved €590 million.

But experts warned that the palace will cost considerably more, in part because the historically accurate reconstruction of the palace's cupola has not been factored into the financing plan. Deutche Welle's (Germany's public broadcasting network) Timothy Rooks gave his opinion: "Tear down Berlin's unfinished airport and start over!

Why can't Berlin finish big public projects? German engineering has become a cliche and they can seemingly build anything on four wheels, but when it comes to four walls it's a different story."

About the Author

Joel D. Joseph is the author of this book. Engine oil has coursed through his veins since he was a teenager. Joseph grew up in Cleveland where his father's company manufactured parts for the Big Three automakers. He learned how to run a milling machine making hubs for torque converters, machining parts, and operating other equipment. Unlike most lawyers, he can take a car apart and put it back together, making it run better.

Joseph, a Georgetown Law grad, was an attorney for Consumers Union, publisher of *Consumer Reports*. He worked with the Center for Auto Safety on improving school bus safety. He is also a class action attorney and has evaluated scores of class action cases against German and other automakers. Joseph has also review safety and recall data from the National Highway Traffic Safety Administration while researching this book.

In 1989, Joseph went to Detroit and met with top Ford Motor Company executives, and the head of the United Auto Workers, and convinced them to put up matching funds to start the Made in the USA Foundation. Their first project was to get the American Automobile

Labeling Act passed. He lobbied, testified before the Senate subcommittee hearing the bill and got it passed.

In the early 1990s Mr. Joseph worked with Warren Brown of the Washington Post and edited his book about the best American cars. Brown's auto column was widely syndicated.

At the Made in the USA Foundation starting in 2010 Joseph created the Made in the USA Hall of Fame. Every year Joseph, as Chairman for the Foundation, gave out 20 awards, three to car companies. Chrysler, Ford, GM and Tesla all have attended.

Joseph, the author of 15 books, wrote **All American Wheels,** a guide to buying American-made cars, trucks and motorcycles for the Made in the USA Foundation.

Mr. Joseph has appeared on all major U.S. television networks promoting his organization and books. His books have been translated and published in the Netherlands, Germany, Japan and other countries.

www.ingramcontent.com/pod-product-compliance
Lightning Source LLC
Chambersburg PA
CBHW051101160426
43193CB00010B/1276